THE HELP

Kathryn Stockett

AUTHORED by Alexandra Nichipor
UPDATED AND REVISED by Aaron Suduiko

COVER DESIGN by Table XI Partners LLC
COVER PHOTO by Olivia Verma and © 2005 GradeSaver, LLC

BOOK DESIGN by Table XI Partners LLC

Published by GradeSaver LLC, www.gradesaver.com

First published in the United States of America by GradeSaver LLC. 2015

ISBN 978-1-60259-578-1

Printed in the United States of America

Table of Contents

Biography of Kathryn Stockett (1969–N/A)

Born in 1969 in Jackson, Mississippi, writer and editor Kathryn Stockett earned her undergraduate degree in English and creative writing from the University of Alabama, then headed to New York City with plans to work in publishing. She spent nine years there, working in magazine publishing and marketing, before moving to Atlanta, Georgia, where she lives with her daughter (she divorced from her husband in 2011). Since moving back to the South, Stockett focused on writing fiction. Her debut novel, *The Help*, was published by Amy Einhorn Books in 2009, and proved to be one of the hit books of the summer season. Like her character Skeeter, Stockett struggled to make her breakthrough as a writer - her manuscript was rejected by over sixty literary agents before finally be accepted by Susan Ramer.

The Help garnered instant attention due to its unusual and rarely addressed subject matter: the relationship in the South between white families and black domestic servants in the 1960s. Having grown up during this period in Mississippi, Stockett was familiar with the dynamic, but nervous about addressing it in a novel, understanding that it was a controversial subject and could result in criticism from both reviewers and from general readers. In an interview with the website Bookreporter, Stockett explained her attitude as a child: "Growing up in Mississippi, almost every family I knew had a black woman working in their house--cooking, cleaning, and taking care of the white children. That was life in Mississippi. I was young and assumed that's how most of America lived." Only after she moved north did Stockett realize that her memories of her childhood were not a universal experience. She found herself reminiscing with other Southerners she met in New York, trading stories about growing up with black domestic help. Gradually, those memories began to spark an idea and she decided to write a story about her relationship with her family's maid when she was a child. Despite being very close to her maid Demetrie, Stockett never stopped to think about what Demetrie's life might be like outside of the work she performed for the white household. She wrote this novel to bridge the gap.

The Help Study Guide

Published in 2009, *The Help* tells the story of three women who work together to challenge the racial status quo of their day. In Jackson Mississippi in the 1960s, aspiring writer Skeeter Phelan gets a dangerous idea: to write a book about what it's really like to be a black maid working for a white family. She enlists the help of Aibileen Clark (a warm, wise black woman with a tragic past) and Minny Jackson (a sharp-tongued maid with a terrible secret) to assist her in this task.

Author Kathryn Stockett drew inspiration for *The Help* (which is her first novel) from her close relationship with her childhood maid, Demetrie. Despite the fact that Demetrie spent so much of her time taking care of the children, Stockett knew very little about her personal life and decided to fill that gap by writing in Demetrie's voice. Demetrie eventually became the character of Aibileen, and Stockett slowly developed the plot for the book.

Stockett had a great deal of trouble in bringing her book to print; over sixty literary agents rejected the manuscript. However, *The Help* has been a resounding commercial success; often described as a "sleeper hit," it has spent two years on the New York Times Bestseller list and sold over five million copies.

Stockett received high praise for her well-developed characters and portrayal of complex social relationships. However, some African-American groups have argued that *The Help* actually exacerbates racism by making the black female characters subordinate to the white main character, Skeeter. Ablene Cooper, a maid who worked for Stockett's brother, sued Stockett for using her life story without permission. However, a Hinds County judge dismissed the case, arguing that the statute of limitations had already passed.

A film based on the novel, directed by Tate Taylor and starring Viola Davis, Octavia Spencer, and Emma Stone, was released in 2011. The film garnered a number of Academy Award nominations, including Best Picture, Best Actress, and Best Supporting Actress.

The Help Summary

The Help focuses on three women in 1960s Jackson Mississippi: Aibileen, who works as a nanny and housekeeper for the Leefolt family; Minny, an outspoken maid; and Skeeter, a recent college graduate. Skeeter longs to pursue a career in writing that will take her beyond the stifling confines of her refined white southern society. Dismayed by the racist Home Help Sanitation Initiative started by her childhood friend Hilly Holbrook, Skeeter starts to think about what it might mean to change attitudes about race in Jackson Mississippi. On the suggestion of Harper and Row editor Elaine Stein, Skeeter starts a dangerous new project: interviewing the maids about what it is like to work as a black maid for a white family. Aibileen and Minny are initially skeptical of this idea, but soon realize that this is an important chance to tell their stories.

Spurred by Hilly's cruel and racist initiatives, the maids of Jackson Mississippi share their stories with Skeeter. Concerned that people will recognize themselves in the book, Minny adds a dark secret about Hilly to the book so that Hilly will stay quiet about the identity of the maids. The book is a surprise hit, generating a great deal of discussion between black and white women. After the success of the novel, Skeeter moves to New York to work in publishing. Aibileen is fired from her job and embarks on a writing career of her own, and Minny leaves her abusive husband.

The Help Characters

Eugenia ("Skeeter") Phelan

The daughter of a wealthy white Southern family, Skeeter is bit of a misfit. Unique among young women in her social circle, she is far more interested in writing than in pursuing marriage and family life. Fixated on her idea of writing a book about the lives of colored maids in Mississippi, she teams up with Aibileen and Minny. She was inspired to write about this topic because of her close relationship with her family's maid Constantine, who disappeared mysteriously shortly before Skeeter came back from college. Skeeter cannot stand hypocrisy and lies, and will often ask difficult and uncomfortable questions.

Aibileen Clark

Aibileen is a gracious, gentle woman who earns her living from taking care of the children of white families, most recently the Leefolt family. She dotes on Mae Mobley, their two-year-old daughter. She still mourns the loss of her son, Treelore, who died in an industrial accident. It is this loss that motivates her to take part on Skeeter's project to document the lives of maids in Mississippi. Aibileen takes primary responsibility for recruiting other maids to work on the project in order to protect her friend Minny.

Minny Jackson

Minny works as a maid, but frequently find herself dismissed from her cleaning jobs due to her sarcastic comments. She has five children whom she loves deeply, but her husband is extremely violent towards her. She starts out working for Miss Walters (Hilly's mother), but when Hilly puts her in a nursing home, Minny finds herself working for Miss Celia, a kind but mysterious outsider with whom she develops a close relationship. She and Hilly are enemies because of the "Terrible Awful" thing that Minny did to Hilly.

Hilly Holbrook

Hilly is a mean-spirited racist and high society southern woman. She is the undisputed leader of the Junior League (a women's organization), and all of the other white women in the town do whatever she says. She is married to William, who is an aspiring politician. She was Skeeter's best childhood friend along with Elizabeth Leefolt, but later events cause a rift between the women.

Celia Foote

Celia is a blond, beautiful, socially outcast woman married to Johnny Foote. Celia was raised in extreme poverty, and her marriage is not only a loving union but also a way to escape this dire economic situation. Minny works for her. Being from such an impoverished background she has never had a maid before, and so she treats Minny with far greater respect that most white women. Celia finds herself rejected from southern society because of her marriage to Johnny (Hilly's ex-boyfriend).

Charlotte Phelan (Skeeter's mother)

Skeeter's mother, Charlotte is an elegant but formidable southern white woman. She is deeply concerned about the fact that her daughter Skeeter did not find a husband in college, and she tries many different strategies to find a match for her daughter. Some of this desperation comes from the fact that she is extremely sick.

Elizabeth Leefolt

Miss Leefolt employs Aibileen to watch over her young daughter, Mae Mobley. She is harsh, icy, and frequently ignores her daughter's pleas for her attention. An angular and vain woman, she was still quite close with Hilly and Skeeter while the three were growing up. She follows Hilly's lead in most difficult situations. She has a difficult relationship with her husband, and the two often fight over money.

Stuart Whitworth

The son of a senator, and Skeeter's boyfriend. Initially, he is heartbroken over a failed engagement to his college girlfriend, Patricia van Devender, and is extremely rude to Skeeter on their first date -- though he later makes up for this, and the two begin a romantic relationship. He is very tall and handsome.

Constantine Bates

Constantine worked as a maid for Skeeter's family, but was mysteriously dismissed by Skeeter's mother. A tall, light-skinned black woman, she doted on Skeeter and was close to her whole family.

William Holbrook

Hilly's husband. He is an aspiring politician, and friends with Stuart Whitworth.

Johnny Foote

Johnny is Celia's husband and Hilly's ex-boyfriend, which leads to a great deal of bad blood between the two women. He is a gentle and kind man, and he loves Celia deeply.

Elaine Stein

Elaine is an editor for Harper & Row Publishing and the person who gives Skeeter the inspiration to write her book about the maids. Elaine is a no-nonsense woman who has been in the publishing business for many years. She is not soft-spoken or gentle, but in her own rough way she encourages Skeeter to push forward with her work.

Mrs. Walters

Mrs. Walters is Hilly's mother, and Minny's employer at the beginning of the book. She is an elderly woman, and very hard of hearing. She shares many traits - vanity, racism, nastiness, etc. - with her daughter Hilly, with whom she has a difficult relationship.

Mae Mobley

Elizabeth Leefolt's young daughter, Mae Mobley is two years old at the beginning of the book. She is curious and sweet, but she is deeply hurt by the fact that her mother never shows her any attention or kindness. She has a very close relationship with Aibileen.

Yule May Crookle

A regal and intelligent woman, Yule May is one of the most educated maids in Jackson, having completed a few years of college before leaving to get married. She is the mother of two twin boys. She was Hilly's maid until she was charged with stealing one of Hilly's rings and sent to jail. The black churches of Jackson put forward the money to send her sons to college.

Lou Anne Templeton

Part of the Junior League, Lou Anne is a society lady. Skeeter has known her for years, but has never found her particularly interesting. However, Lou Anne has a very close relationship with her maid, Louvenia, who supports Lou Anne through her bouts of severe depression and her suicide attempts. In return, Lou Anne helps Louvenia take care of her grandson, who was severely injured in a racially motivated attack.

Louvenia

A black maid known for her sweet nature. She works for Lou Anne Templeton, with whom she has a very close relationship. Her grandson Robert was beaten and blinded by white men.

The Help Glossary

Amicable

Friendly; without disagreement or rancor.

Antebellum

Referring to the historical period in the American south before the Civil War; literally meaning 'before war'.

Auburn

A dark red-brown.

Chateaubriand

A type of thick steak, cut from the tenderloin.

Chifforobe

A stand-alone piece of furniture in which one hangs clothes; a wardrobe.

Corn pone

Another name for corn bread; a type of sweet bread containing corn.

Defoliant

A chemical that strips the leaves from plants and trees.

Degustationary

Characterized by careful, appreciative tasting of food.

Fiddleheads

A small shoot from an edible type of fern. Its name comes from its resemblance to the curled top of a fiddle.

Fie

An expression of disgust or outrage.

Gentility

Good manners, behavior, and appearance; social superiority.

Grits

A popular southern dish, made of ground corn, whole milk, and cheese.

High Cotton

Doing well, being successful.

High Yellow

Slang term for a light-skinned black child.

Huarache shoes

Light, woven sandals.

Insipid

Lacking vigor; uninteresting.

Jelly-rolling

Slang term for sexual activity.

Law

When spoken by Minny or Aibileen, this word means "Lord"; used to express great emotion.

Kudzu

Long trailing vines; they grow in tangled bunches on trees.

Taffeta

A smooth, plan fabric, often used for ball gowns.

The Help Themes

Race and Racism

Racism manifests in the lives of the black maids in a number of ways: they are denied opportunities for educational or professional advancement, they perform repetitive work for white families, they must curtail their speech to prevent violence, and they must use separate facilities. Perhaps most damaging of all, black people are constantly exposed to social messages telling them that they are dirty, lazy, and in all respects less than white people.

Even the way the book is written hearkens back to this central theme. When writing from the perspective of the black maids Aibileen and Minny, Stockett uses an antiquated form of speech. While this is meant to lend authenticity to their voices, it also makes them sound uneducated and makes it somewhat difficult to relate to them.

The Help also suggests that it is possible to cross this racial divide. In addition to anecdotes about rude or abusive employers, we hear stories of maids who have very close relationships with the white families for whom they work. Through her efforts to be a mouthpiece for the black maids of Jackson, Skeeter develops a close friendship with Aibileen and Minny. It's possible, through effort and understanding, to begin to heal the wounds of racism.

Mothers and Daughters

Mothers and daughters have difficult but deeply loving relationships. *The Help* examines several different types of mother-daughter relationships.

Elizabeth Leefolt has a strained relationship with her mother, who is aloof and demanding; she continues this unhealthy dynamic by being neglectful and critical of her own daughter, Mae Mobley. There's also an indication that mother-daughter relationships are not necessarily dependent on blood ties. For example, Aibileen acts as a mother to Mae Mobley, not only taking care of her day-to-day needs but also teaching her to be kind to others and to always have respect for herself.

Skeeter has a difficult but loving relationship with her mother, who is constantly pressuring her daughter to dress better and catch a man. Skeeter later discovers that this critical edge is tempered by love; her mother has cancer, and she wants to make sure her daughter has a good life after she is gone. Though Skeeter's mother often bosses her daughter, she also stands up for her at critical moments, such as during her conflicts with Hilly and Stuart.

Love and Friendship

The Help takes a close look at many types of love, some of them unlikely and fraught with difficulties. The close bond between black caretakers and white children (Aibileen and Mae Mobley, as well as Skeeter and Constantine) show that nurturing love is not limited to blood relationships. As we see later in the book, this bond is often unfairly complicated by the strictures of a racist society.

Because of her new consciousness regarding race, Skeeter causes a rupture in her friendships with Hilly and Elizabeth Leefolt. Through a series of events (the discovery of the Jim Crow materials, the toilet prank, Hilly's comment about Stuart), these lifelong friendships are torn apart. But we also see how new friendships can emerge out of the ashes of old ones: it is Aibileen and Minny with whom Skeeter celebrates her new job in New York City.

The novel also focuses on different types of romantic love. Despite his affection for Skeeter, Stuart cannot get over the betrayal of his fiancée, Patricia van Devender, and his attempts to build a new relationship with Skeeter continuously fail. On the other hand, Celia and Johnny have a deeply loving relationship, triumphing over class differences, infertility, and social disapproval.

A Writer's Life

What does it mean to be a writer? The journey to publish the book is not an easy one. After an initial stroke of luck in catching Elaine Stein's attention, Skeeter struggles to develop her ideas, conduct interviews, write the book, and find a publisher. Each step is fraught with difficulties; for example, she must complete the book in only a few weeks in order to send it in for the annual editor's meeting. Skeeter spends many long nights typing until her hands are covered with ink and paper cuts, but she ultimately prevails.

Skeeter is not the only prospective writer in the book. Despite her academic excellence, Aibileen was forced to drop out of school to support her family. However, she writes down her prayers every day, continuing to build her skills in writing. Assisting Skeeter with the book about the maids gives her the chance to showcase her writing skills, and she eventually becomes the first black author of the Miss Myrna column. At the end of the novel, she thinks about developing her writing career even more.

Being a Woman

The varying difficulties faced by women constitute another major theme in the book. In the workplace, Minny struggles with the possibility of being fired due to her outspoken personality; at home, she is violently abused by her husband. Aibileen must cope with the sorrow of her son's untimely death at the same time that she tries to support the neglected Mae Mobley. Skeeter is struggling with a world that does not value her professional ambitions and tries to force her into the narrow roles of wife and mother. Celia Foote deals with a series of miscarriages and her social isolation, which is worsened by her desire to be a capable wife to her beloved husband. Each of these women struggle to overcome these difficulties, but they also forge close bonds with other women over shared problems.

Doing the Right Thing

Even when everything in the world is trying to tell you what to do and what to believe, you need to make your own path. The central protagonists recognize that the current state of race relations is wrong, and work to correct it. Aibileen strives to teach racial equality and acceptance to Mae Mobley. Minny persists in working on the book about the maids despite the danger it puts her in with her own husband and Hilly. Skeeter continues working towards racial justice despite the rift it causes between her and her two best friends.

Southern Values

The Help is a window onto the mid-century south, giving the reader vivid impressions of the beautiful landscapes and warm culture. This includes positive qualities such as friendliness and generosity; we see these close social ties in the ways that family members treat one another. Yet it also includes racism, segregation, and misogyny, which are evident in the violent enforcement of the separation between races, and the lack of professional options for white women.

The Help Quotes and Analysis

> *"'I use my colored bathroom from now on. And then I go on and Clorox the white bathroom again real good.'"*

pg. 14

Aibileen says this to Miss Leefolt after she installs a second bathroom for the "colored help," as Hilly had suggested. Miss Leefolt tells Aibileen about the new bathroom, and asks her to go try it out. Aibileen responds with this comment, which exemplifies the paradoxical and contradictory nature of race relations at that time: it is perfectly acceptable for a black woman to clean up after a white family or to care for their children, but it is unacceptable for her to use the same facilities as them.

> *"Even though I felt miserable, and knew that I was most likely ugly, it was the first time she had ever talked to me like I was something besides my mother's white child. All my life I'd been told what to believe about politics, coloreds, being a girl. But with Constantine's thumb pressed in my hand, I realized I actually had a choice what I could believe."*

pg. 74

Skeeter is reduced to tears after a boy calls her ugly when she was thirteen years old. Constantine tells her that true ugliness is being a mean and hurtful person, and that every day Skeeter must ask herself if she will choose to believe the nonsense that other people say about her. This is the critical moment in the relationship between Skeeter and Constantine, and it plants a rebellious streak in Skeeter's heart. She will not be blindly bigoted against colored people, she will not accept that a white woman's only role in life is to get married and have children. Instead, she will work to forge her own path and live by her own values.

> *"Write about what disturbs you, particularly if it bothers no one else."*

pg. 83

Elaine Stein offers this piece of advice in the letter she writes to Skeeter. Skeeter takes this advice to heart, and starts thinking about her bond with Constantine and the ugly harassment of black maids she says every day, ultimately deciding to write her book about the maids. It is also the guiding maxim of *The Help* itself, which covers many situations (racism, sexism, miscarriages, domestic violence) that are disturbing.

> *"Mae Mobley," I say cause I got a notion to try something. "You a smart girl?"*
>
> *She just look at me, like she don't know.*

"You a smart girl," I say again.

She say, "Mae Mo smart."

I say, "You a kind little girl?"

She just look at me. She two years old. She don't know what she is yet.

I say, "You a kind girl," and she nod, repeat it back to me. But before I can do another one, sheb get up and chase that poor dog around the yard and laugh and that's when I get to wondering, what would happen if I told her she something good, every day?

pg. 107

Dismayed by how Miss Leefolt only speaks to Mae Mobley in order to scold her, Aibileen decides to tell Mae Mobley that she is smart and kind every day. Aibileen has raised seventeen white children, and she knows that children are shaped by the world around them and the values that they imbibe. This quote is an example of the close and loving relationship between black caregivers and white children.

"'I'd like to write this showing the point of view of the help. The colored women down here.' I tried to picture Constantine's face, Aibileen's. 'They raise a white child and then twenty years later the child becomes the employer. It's that irony, that we love them and they love us, yet...' I swallowed, my voice trembling. 'We don't even allow them to use the toilet in the house.'"

pg. 125

Elaine Stein has phoned Skeeter asking about her ideas, and Skeeter is explaining her interest in writing a book about what it is like to be a black maid in Mississippi. Skeeter is haunted by Constantine's mysterious disappearance, and she is also growing close with Aibileen, who gives her tips for the Miss Myrna cleaning column. This quote reveals Skeeter's more altruistic reasons for writing her book on maids: she wants to use her social privilege to give voice to the black women she has been close to in her life.

"Thirty-five maids done said no and I feel like I'm selling something nobody want to buy. Something big and stinky, like Kiki Brown and her lemon smell-good polish. But what really makes me and Kiki the same is, I'm proud a what I'm selling. I can't help it. We telling stories that need to be told."

pg. 244

Aibileen, who was suspicious of Skeeter's project at first, is now convinced of its importance. Despite the fact that thirty-five women have refused to participate, she's still hopeful that she can drum up some interest in this important project. She compares herself to another woman at the church who tries (mostly unsuccessfully) to sell her homemade cleaning products. This is the moment when we see that Aibileen truly believes in the importance of writing the book about the maids.

> *"It is 1963. The Space Age they're calling it. A man has circled the earth in a rocketship. They've invented a pill so married women don't have to get pregnant. A can of beer opens with a single finger instead of a can opener. Yet my parents' house is still as hot as it was in 1899, the year my Great-grandfather built it."*
>
> *pg. 280*

These musings begin one of Skeeter's chapters, highlighting two aspects of life in the south: the adherence to tradition and the sweltering heat. The quote points to one of the central contradictions of the 1960s: the United States was making enormous technological strides, but race relations had remained largely unchanged for nearly a century. Even though rocket ships circled the earth, there were still separate bathrooms for whites and people of color. The point also hints at another aspect of the conflict between Skeeter (who desperately wants air-conditioning in the house) and her mother (who finds such equipment to be tacky).

> *"My boys are equally as smart, equally eager for an education. But we only had the money for one and I ask you, how do you choose which of your twin sons should go to college and which should take a job spreading tar? How do you tell one that you love him just as much as the other, but you've decided he won't be the one to get a chance in life? You don't. You find a way to make it happen. Any way at all."*
>
> *Pg. 294*

After she is imprisoned for stealing Hilly's ring, Yule May writes this letter to Skeeter to explaining her motivations. This quote demonstrates the impossible and agonizing situation for black mothers in this time and place, many of whom had multiple children and could not afford to send them all to school. The letter also leads Skeeter to conclude it was more wrong for Hilly to send Yule May to prison than it was for Yule May was to steal Hilly's ring, which eventually leads to the end of the friendship between Hilly and Skeeter.

> *There is undisguised hate for white women, there is inexplicable love. Faye Belle, palsied and gray-skinned, cannot remember her own age. Her stories unfold like soft linen. She remembers hiding in a steamer trunk with a little white girl while Yankee soldiers stomped through the house. Twenty years ago, she held that same white girl, by then an old woman, in her arms while she died. Each proclaimed their love as best friends. Swore that death would not change this. That color meant nothing. The white woman's grandson still pays Faye Belle's rent. When she's feeling strong, Faye Belle sometimes goes over and cleans up his kitchen.*

Pg. 303

Though this story comes from an elderly black maid, we hear it through the voice of Skeeter (who at this point is wise enough to describe the love between a black and white woman as inexplicable). Examples of white women being rude, discriminatory, or exploitative of their black maids are not difficult to find in the pages of The Help, but this is a potent example of a close and loving relationship between a black woman and a white one. It is a hint that friendship can flourish despite color divide, and that such friendship can forge ties between the generations; the woman's grandson still makes sure that Faye Belle lives comfortably.

> *"'I used to be a good fighter.' She looks out along the boxwoods, wipes off her sweat with her palm. 'If you'd known me ten years ago....'*
>
> *She's got no goo on her face, her hair's not sprayed, her nightgown's like an old prairie dress. She takes a deep breath through her nose and I see it. I see the white-trash girl she was ten years ago. She was strong. She didn't take no shit from nobody.*

Pg. 365

This quote comes from Minny, who makes this observation immediately after Celia drives away the crazed naked man who tried to attack them both. It offers us a view of Celia quite different than the passive, pink-clad, empty-headed one we've known, showcasing her strength and her difficult past. It also marks the moment when Minny truly comes to respect and like Celia. She notes that Celia has the same personality characteristics that she prides in herself: strength and a refusal to take 'shit' from anyone else.

> *"'Well, Hilly's that what you get, I guess. And I wouldn't go tattling on Minny either, or you'll be known all over town as the lady who ate two slices of Minny's shit.'"*

Pg. 399

This quote is spoken by Miss Walters (Hilly's mother) immediately after the Terrible Awful, summing up the act itself. It is significant that Miss Walter's relationship with her daughter Hilly is so strained that she isn't even concerned about her daughter when she eats a pie containing feces.

> *Wasn't that the point of the book? For women to realize, We are just two people. Not that much separates us. Not nearly as much as I'd thought.*

Pg. 492

Skeeter thinks this after her meeting with Lou Anne in the drugstore. Lou Anne has figured out which chapter was Louvenia speaking about her, and she is deeply touched by the kind things Louvenia said about her. Despite pressure from Hilly, Lou

Anne swears that she will never fire Louvenia, who has supported her through her depression. Skeeter is surprised to hear these fierce words from Lou Anne, whom she has always considered rather dull. This prompts Skeeter to consider how much she had underestimated not only Lou Anne, but also the many women she spoke to over the course of writing the book. Kathryn Stockett has cited this quote as the central message of *The Help*.

The Help Chapter 1 - 4 Summary and Analysis

Summary:

Chapter 1

(Written from the perspective of Aibileen.) Still in mourning for her son Treelore (who died in an industrial accident), Aibileen dotes on the sweet-natured Mae Mobley, daughter of a white family. However, she dislikes her employer Miss Leefolt, who is icy, harsh, and frequently neglects her daughter.

One day, Miss Leefolt invites several guests over for a game of cards: Hilly, Hilly's mother Mrs. Walters, and Skeeter. Hilly comments that Mrs. Walters - who employs Aibileen's best friend Minny as a cook and maid - is looking sick and skinny, remarking that Minny must not be doing her job. Aibileen grows anxious because few families will hire Minny due to her sharp tongue and tendency to make sarcastic comments; Mrs. Walters is not bothered by this habit because she is nearly deaf. Hilly also reveals her plan to require all white homes to have separate bathrooms for the black maids, which she claims is necessary to prevent disease. Skeeter reacts to this suggestion with obvious disgust, and later asks Aibileen in private if she has ever wanted to change things. Miss Leefolt walks in before Aibileen can answer, but this peculiar encounter continues to haunt Aibileen.

Chapter 2

(Written from the perspective of Aibileen.) The next day Minny calls Aibileen and says that Hilly is sending her mother, Mrs. Walters, to a retirement home. Minny panics that she will be without a job, and her worry intensifies when she finds out Hilly has spread rumors that Minny is a thieving maid. The Leefolt family - Aibileen's employers - argue about the expensive involved in adding another bathroom for the help to use, and Miss Leefolt slaps Mae Mobley when she pulls on the phone cord trying to get her mother's attention. That night at home, Aibileen writes down her prayers as she always does, and she finds herself adding Skeeter to the list for reasons she cannot explain. Minny insists that Aibileen's prayer list has special powers to protect those on it.

The next day, Celia Foote calls Miss Leefolt's house, and Aibileen picks up. Celia says she is looking to speak to Miss Leefolt about the Children's Benefit. Aibileen knows that Hilly and Miss Leefolt hate Celia because she married Hilly's ex-boyfriend Johnny. When Celia mentions she's looking for a recommendation for home help, Aibileen is quick to suggest her friend Minny. She lies to Celia, saying that Miss Leefolt has told her to keep this recommendation a secret because all Miss Leefolt's friends want to hire Minny. Aibileen then phones Minny, who is delighted about this new job opportunity.

Chapter 3

(Written from the perspective of Minny.) Minny nervously arrives at the home of Celia Foote, a blonde woman who resembles Marilyn Monroe. Minny is somewhat suspicious when Celia asks her if she'd like to sit down and have a glass of water - no white woman ever offers such courtesy to the colored help. Minny quickly discovers that this is because of Celia's impoverished background growing up in rural Mississippi.

Celia expresses concern that the house will be too much for Minny to clean, but Minny insists she can do it. Celia says that she cannot tell her husband that she has hired a maid, because she wants him to think that she is "worth the trouble" (pg. 44). She also asks Minny to give her cooking lessons. Minny points out that if Celia's husband finds a black woman in his kitchen he is likely to shoot her, but Celia offers Minny such high pay and such reasonable hours that Minny finally agrees to the arrangement.

Minny thinks back to her childhood, when her mother told her the rules for working in white homes: stay out of their business, use separate bathroom facilities and eating utensils, and never talk back to your employers. It's usually the third rule that's hardest for Minny, but lately she's been spending a lot of time puzzling over Celia's life. Celia mostly sits around and reads magazines all day, getting up only to use the bathroom or eat her meals. Most peculiarly, they have no children, despite the fact that they have been married for some time.

Chapter 4

(Written from the perspective of Minny.) Minny appreciates her well-paying job working for the Foote family, but she puzzles over the mysterious Celia, who speaks wistfully about her love for gardening but refuses to step outside. It becomes clear that Celia cannot iron or clean (she buys new shirts for her husband so that he won't notice this), and Minny must painstakingly teach her how to cook even the simplest meals. Still she doesn't dislike Celia; the woman is kind and seems a bit lonely, because the other white socialites in town refuse to return her phone calls. When Minnie sees a picture of Celia's husband, she realizes why - Celia has married Hilly's ex-boyfriend, Johnny.

Minny hates the fact that Celia refuses to tell her husband that she has hired a maid, though Celia promises to tell him in a few months. One day when Johnny comes home early, Minny has to hide in the spare bathroom to avoid detection.

Analysis:

The three main protagonists (Aibileen, Skeeter, and Minny) take turns narrating the story; the first two chapters are told from Aibileen's point of view. In order to lend authenticity to the novel, the author uses a form of African-American vernacular English when writing from the perspectives of Minny and Aibileen. Though this technique is meant to give a unique voice to these women, it also results in grammatically incorrect or confusing sentences, which may be puzzling to some readers. It may be helpful to read some sentences out loud, so that the reader can hear what they sound like spoken.

The first four chapters vividly convey the daily indignities of being black in the segregated south. For example, Hilly Holbrook suggests that black people should have to use different bathrooms in white homes because she believes they carry disease, and she says this while Aibileen is present. Hilly does not care how much she offends any black person.

Life as a maid is precarious and difficult. Aibileen must clean the house every day while she also takes care of little Mae Mobley, and this leaves her little time to focus on her own life. Minny, on the other hand, struggles with the consequences of speaking her mind while also being a provider to her five children. As Minny discovers when Hilly decides to send her mother to a nursing home, being a maid is a position with absolutely no job security; a maid can be fired at any time for any infraction, and despite years of service, she might find it difficult to find another position if someone in the white community spreads rumors about her.

The novel also highlights the tender and loving relationships between caregivers and children. Aibileen cares deeply about Mae Mobley, paying much more attention to her than her mother does, and putting her first on her prayer list. Aibileen is infuriated at the cold way Miss Leefolt treats Mae Mobley (slapping her when she tries to get her mother's attention), but Aibileen cannot rebuke her employer; she can only offer love and tenderness to Mae Mobley.

The appearance of Celia Foote introduces class conflict to the previous themes of gender and race. Though she is white, Celia grew up in an impoverished community and has no experience bossing around people of color. This is evidenced by her awkwardness in asking Minny how much she would like to be paid and when she would like to work. Celia adores her husband but also fears him, because he belongs to a social class far above hers and is the reason that she has been pulled out of her childhood poverty. She wants to hide the fact that she has hired Minny because she wants her husband to believe that she is a capable wife and housekeeper.

The Help Chapters 5 - 7 Summary and Analysis

Summary:

Chapter 5

(Written from Skeeter's point of view.) A college graduate who has recently moved back to her parents' home, Skeeter is facing a number of difficulties. She is hurt and angry about her best friend Hilly's threat to kick her out of the League, which indicates just how far apart the two women have grown. Skeeter's mother is concerned that her daughter has not gotten married yet at the late age of twenty-three, so she constantly nags Skeeter to do whatever she can to get a man. Skeeter, however, is much more interested in finding a job where she can pursue her passion for writing. The only job to which she has applied (an editor position at Harper & Row) has not gotten back to her. Flipping through the employment listings in the local paper, Skeeter notices that many jobs offer women lower pay than men for the same work.

Skeeter misses her childhood maid, Constantine, who was mysteriously dismissed from the household during Skeeter's senior year of college. Skeeter reminisces about her close relationship with Constantine, remembering a time when a boy called her ugly and Constantine comforted her by saying that true ugliness comes from being a mean and spiteful person. Skeeter's mother constantly harangued her to brush her hair or wear more flattering clothes, but Constantine was interested in what Skeeter's thoughts and ideas. Still, Skeeter understands that there's much about Constantine's life that she doesn't know; for example, Constantine once casually mentioned that her father is white, which surprises Skeeter and raises a number of questions. Skeeter and Constantine remained close even when Skeeter goes off to college, writing letters to each other frequently. In Constantine's last letter to Skeeter, she mentions that she has a surprise for her, but Skeeter's mother says that Constantine left to live with her people up in Chicago. Skeeter is certain that there is more to the story than this.

Chapter 6

(Written from Skeeter's perspective.) One September morning, Skeeter is delighted to see that she has received a reply from Harper & Row. She hasn't gotten the job, but one of the editors, Elaine Stein, has decided to give her some career advice. Stein tells Skeeter that she should get an entry-level job at a newspaper, and should write about the things that disturb her. She offers to read some of Skeeter's ideas as well, and Skeeter sends her a list of topics such as drunk driving, illiteracy, and so on. Skeeter heads to the Jackson Journal, asking about any reporter positions that they have open. Though the editor, Mr. Golden, is rather rude (he asks if she managed to have any fun in college), he offers her a position writing Miss Myrna's weekly cleaning advice column.

Skeeter is elated with her new job, but her mother comments about how ironic it is that Skeeter - who has never cleaned anything in her life - is writing a cleaning column. Her mother is dismayed that this job will give Skeeter no opportunities to meet a potential husband. Skeeter realizes that her mother is right about her lack of knowledge of cleaning, and decides to ask her friend Elizabeth Leefolt's maid, Aibileen, some questions about cleaning in order to write the column. Elizabeth grudgingly allows this, and so Aibileen answers Skeeter's questions about scrubbing bathtubs and getting stains out of clothing. Skeeter casually mentions Constantine and how she moved up to Chicago, but Aibileen says that Skeeter's mother fired Constantine. Skeeter confronts her mother about this, and her mother refuses to explain further, saying only that Skeeter will understand when she hires help of her own.

Skeeter continues asking Aibileen about cleaning advice for her column, and the two begin to grow close. Aibileen casually mentions Constantine's very light-skinned daughter, who appeared at Skeeter's mother's house shortly before Constantine was fired. Aibileen stops herself and says she is scared to say anything more.

Skeeter receives a reply from Elaine Stein, who is not impressed by her dull and passionless list of ideas. Skeeter is devastated, but she also realizes that she should have chosen ideas that interest her rather than ideas that sound impressive. The seed of an idea begins to grow in her mind, a dangerous but compelling one that won't go away....

Chapter 7

(Written from Aibileen's perspective.) Little Mae Mobley is growing up fast, and Aibileen reminisces about her other "used-to-be" babies while Mae plays in the yard. Mae Mobley's mother steps in to snap at her for not eating in her high chair, and Mae Mobley calls herself a bad girl. Aibileen denies this, and tells Mae that she is smart and kind; she prompts her to repeat this and remember it.

Aibileen realizes it's time to potty-train Mae Mobley. This is made more difficult by the fact that Miss Leefolt refuses to let Mae Mobley watch her using the toilet, which would set an example for the young girl to follow. Mae has a great deal of trouble figuring out how to use the toilet, so Aibileen realizes that she will have to show the girl what to do. Aibileen faces a conundrum: show Mae Mobley on the white toilet, or on the "colored toilet" in the garage set aside for the black maids? She decides that the best course of action is to take the girl to the colored toilet; Aibileen sits down and uses the toilet. After she is done, Mae immediately jumps up and uses the toilet herself for the first time, to Aibileen's great pride.

When Miss Leefolt comes home, Aibileen proudly tells her that Mae Mobley has learned to use the toilet. Eager to show her mother, Mae runs to the bathroom...the "colored" bathroom in the garage. Miss Leefolt flies into a rage, spanking her daughter harshly, and telling her never to use that bathroom because it is dirty and diseased.

Aibileen continues to give Skeeter information about cleaning for her newspaper column, and she finds herself talking to Skeeter about things she has never spoken to any white person about, such as the politics of her church or her son Treelore's excellent grades. Still, she can't bring herself to talk to Skeeter on the third anniversary of Treelore's tragic death.

But life goes on. Aibileen goes grocery shopping to supply the Leefolt family's Thanksgiving, and while there she runs into another maid who tells her about another tragic event: a young black man named Robert (who is the grandson of Louvenia, one of the matriarchs of the black community) used an unlabeled white restroom, and two white men beat him with a tire iron until he was blind in one eye. Aibileen is horrified.

Aibileen is shocked to find Skeeter waiting for her when she gets home. Skeeter says she wants to interview Aibileen about what it's like to be a maid, and what it's like to work for a white family. Aibileen says that this is extremely dangerous, and points out the violence meted to black people who challenge the status quo, most recently Louvenia's grandson. Skeeter asks her to think about it, but Aibileen says no and walks away.

Analysis:

Thus far we have mainly heard the about the difficulties faced by black women (which are substantial), but chapters 5 and 6 indicate that white women also face some difficulties. Though she is only twenty-three, Skeeter is under enormous pressure to marry; all of her friends have done so, her mother is constantly badgering her about getting a boyfriend. Skeeter knows that marriage will mean the end of her professional ambitions, and moreover, it will mean subordinating her intellect to that of her husband. But though she tries to avoid marriage, her family, friends, and society do not let her forget that she will be considered a failure until she marries.

As a woman, Skeeter's position in the white world is inferior. She is discouraged from getting a job despite her education and talents, and she discovers that she will be paid less than a man for performing the same work. When she appears for a job interview at the local paper, she receives inappropriate comments from the managing editor about her appearance and social activities. She persists despite this disrespect, and manages to get a minor position writing a column about women's work. Still, it's a start.

Despite her gender, Skeeter still has a great deal of power over the maids. She essentially plagiarizes Aibileen's experience to write her column and doesn't think twice about it. However, Skeeter also begins to question some of the things she has been taught since childhood, such as the idea that black people are all dirty and diseased.

Chapters 5 and 7 offer the reader a more detailed perspective on the relationship between black maids and the white children they raise. Skeeter treasures her memories of Constantine, and had a more loving relationship with her than she did with her own mother. However, Skeeter is stunned to learn that Constantine had a daughter; despite their close relationship, Constantine never felt safe telling Skeeter about this major aspect of her personal life. Though maids might seem to be family or even closer than family, this is still a tenuous economic arrangement that does not favor the maids. The black women are dependent for their livelihood on this work, whereas white families know they can always hire another maid.

The black maids struggle with having so little official influence over the children they care for; this is made clear through the relationship between Aibileen and Mae Mobley. After Miss Leefolt spanks her daughter for using the colored bathroom, Aibileen feels deep guilt for indirectly causing harm to the girl, but she also hates that Mae Mobley is being taught to believe that black people are dirty and diseased. Aibileen is responsible for daily activities like feeding, cleaning, and playing with Mae Mobley, and she is the one the girl spends most of her time with. However, she has absolutely no control over the major decisions in Mae's life, and she has a limited capacity to instill important values.

The vicious beating perpetrated against Louvenia's grandson marks a major turning point in the narrative. We begin to see an indication that racism can be even more serious than separate bathroom facilities or snide remarks from employers - racism can literally kill. Dread of similar treatment will haunt all of the black characters throughout the rest of the novel. They know very well that the price for challenging racism can be violence or death.

The Help Chapters 8 - 10 Summary and Analysis

Summary:

Chapter 8

(Written from the perspective of Skeeter.) Skeeter is dismayed that Aibileen does not want to be part of the book about the lives of black maids in Mississippi. This is a problem for Skeeter because she has already told Elaine Stein from Harper and Row that she's found a maid to interview. Elaine is intrigued by this idea, and calls up Skeeter to discuss it with her. Skeeter says she got this idea from being raised by Constantine, a colored woman. Elaine points out that race and integration are the hottest topics in the nation right now, but a black maid working for a white family is putting herself in extreme danger by openly discussing her experiences. Still, Skeeter is determined to forge ahead with this idea.

A few days later, Skeeter meets with Aibileen again to ask her more questions for the Miss Myrna cleaning column. Skeeter also offers Aibileen five dollars for every article she has helped with, but Aibileen refuses the money, explaining that Miss Leefolt would not like it and that Aibileen will not help Skeeter with her book. Skeeter leaves embarrassed.

Skeeter's mother buys her a peculiar machine called the Magic Soft & Silky Shinalator, which is supposed to tame Skeeter's curly hair for her date with a senator's son. To their amazement, the machine actually works.

Chapter 9

(Written from the perspective of Skeeter.) The day of Skeeter's date with Stuart Whitworth, the senator's son, has finally arrived. Hilly has set them up together. With a new dress and shiny straight hair, Skeeter heads into the date full of hope...which is quickly frustrated.

Because she has decided to hide the date from her parents, Skeeter has to take a tractor to Hilly's house, and she arrives extremely late to find Stuart sipping drinks in the kitchen with Hilly and her husband. Skeeter, Stuart, Hilly, and Hilly's husband head out for dinner, and Stuart orders a whiskey. Noticing Johnny Foote and his wife Celia, Stuart comments on how attractive she is, much to Skeeter's anger. He then goes on to mock her work writing the Miss Myrna cleaning column, saying that the only thing more boring than housework is writing about housework, and this all must be an elaborate ploy to snag a husband, anyway. Skeeter asks him if he was dropped on his head as a child. Hilly and her husband keep things civil, but Stuart gets more and more deeply drunk. After they leave, Hilly's husband asks Skeeter to give Stuart a ride home, because he is too drunk to drive. Stuart makes a rude comment about

Skeeter's tractor and she bursts into tears. Stuart apologizes half-heartedly, saying he was just never ready for this date.

Still recovering from this disappointment, Skeeter receives a phone call from Aibileen, who has decided to speak about her experiences as a black maid; she does insist on precautions such as changing names and meeting in the colored neighborhood so that they will not be overheard. Skeeter feels a bit of apprehension as she realizes that by interviewing Aibileen she will be rooting out her friend Elizabeth Leefolt's secrets, but does not let this occupy her thoughts. Skeeter asks Aibileen what made her change her mind on this matter, and Aibileen replies with two words - Miss Hilly.

Chapter 10

(Written from the perspective of Minny.) The first of December has come, and Celia has still not told her husband that she is receiving home help from Minny. Minny is anxious: will Celia's husband fire her, kill her, or thank her for all of the work she's done? Celia seems as frightened as Minny about the prospect of Celia's husband coming home early. Minny is also tired of Celia taking credit for all her good cooking; despite Minny's lessons, Celia's cooking skills have not improved. Despite her best efforts to ingratiate herself into the town's social circles, Celia still finds that her phone calls go unanswered because of her marriage to Johnny, Hilly's ex-boyfriend.

Aibileen gives Minny strange news: Skeeter is writing a book about the experiences of black maids in Mississippi, and Aibileen is going to help her by telling her own story - and she wants Minny to do so too. The idea is exciting to Minny (finally, a chance to speak her mind and to tell the truth!), but she thinks it's absolutely crazy.

One day while Minny is working in the kitchen, she noticed Celia turn pale and break out into a sweat; she snaps at Celia and then asks her to bring a glass of water, two things that she has never done before. Minny wonders if this is related to Celia's frequent, sneaky trips upstairs. The next day, Celia refuses to get out of bed, then runs to the bathroom suddenly and yells at Minny to leave.

Celia apologizes the next day, explaining that she was feeling poorly. But just a few days before Celia is supposed to tell Johnny that Minny is helping her keep house, Johnny comes home early and sees Minny. She's terrified, but he just laughs and says it's fine - he had a feeling there was help around because the cooking suddenly became delicious. Johnny says that Celia is determined to do things for him by herself, and that was part of the reason that she was so reluctant to tell him. He's worried about his wife, noticing that she doesn't seem happy, and asks Minny what she thinks he should do. Minny does not have an answer for this. Johnny says that he's trying to get his friend Will to make his wife Hilly spend more time with Celia, but to know avail. Minny is suddenly terrified that the Terrible Awful thing she did to Hilly will follow her even here.

Analysis:

So far Skeeter has been remarkable because of her consciousness regarding race and her strong-minded determination to be a writer. Chapters 8 and 9 reveal another side of Skeeter: her naiveté. She understands that black maids might be wary about being interviewed, but she does not comprehend the extreme danger that this project puts them in. She offers Aibileen money for her help in writing the cleaning column, but she is not sensitive enough to realize that Aibileen sees this as a bribe to participate in the book about the maids. Additionally, Skeeter has no idea how hazardous it would be for a black maid to be caught with a stack of money in her place of employment.

Still, Skeeter also starts to become a little bit more sensitive to the indignities endured by the black maids. At one point, Hilly pressures Aibileen into saying thank you for building her separate bathroom; only Skeeter notices how Aibileen hangs her head in disgust. Aibileen recognizes that this book project is perhaps the only way she has to safely challenge the racism of the south and to tell her story. Deeply angered by Hilly's bullying, Aibileen decides to throw in her lot with Skeeter.

Skeeter's interaction with Stuart develops the themes of love and relationships. Stuart is insensitive, rude, and possibly an alcoholic...but he is taller than Skeeter and he comes from a good family, so he's considered a catch. Still, even Skeeter cannot stand the way that he insults her at every turn, mocking her ambition and saying she is working only to get a husband. Skeeter is not terribly optimistic about the date from the beginning; she hides this date from her mother so that Mrs. Phelan won't be disappointed when it inevitably fails.

In Chapter 10, Aibileen starts to organize the other maids to contribute to the book, beginning with her friend Minny. Minny is excited about the idea, but she is also deeply afraid to put herself and her family in danger by speaking out. Given the power that white people wield over blacks, the increasing frequency of violence against outspoken blacks, and Skeeter's personal self-interest, it's hard to blame Minny for her suspicions.

Celia's circumstances grow more mysterious. What is her illness? Why does she sit around the house so much? Why does she take frequent sneaky trips upstairs? Her husband Johnny's discovery of Minny is fortunately uneventful; he already guessed that his wife hired a maid, and meeting Minny just confirmed this. However, he does request that Minny refrain from telling Celia that he knows she has hired a maid, because he doesn't want to hurt his wife's feelings. Though Celia and Johnny clearly have a loving marriage, they seem to suffer from a lack of communication.

The Help Chapters 11 - 13 Summary and Analysis

Summary:

Chapter 11

(Written from the perspective of Skeeter.) Skeeter secretively heads to Aibileen's house to interview her for the book. She poses a number of rather dull questions to Aibileen: when was she born, did she always know she would be a maid? Aibileen provides short and unproductive answers for all of these questions, but she is caught off guard when Skeeter asks her what she dislikes most about her job. Aibileen rushes out of the room, and then returns apologizing, saying she thought she was ready to talk but she just needs to lie down for now. Dismayed, Skeeter leaves.

A few days later, Skeeter receives a message from Aibileen, who has realized that writing her own story will help her feel more comfortable answering questions. Skeeter is skeptical of this idea at first, saying that writing isn't easy, but Aibileen argues that it is not so different from writing her prayers every night. Aibileen reads aloud what she has written: being fired for miscounting the silverware, taking a white boy to a colored hospital out of desperation, and so on. Skeeter types her worlds, and is incredibly impressed with Aibileen's beautiful prose.

Chapter 12

(Written from the perspective of Skeeter.) Aibileen tells more of her life story to Skeeter: the children she has cared for, the cotton-picking she has done, and her thoughts on the separate bathroom policy. Aibileen explains the circumstances of Treelore's death: the white foreman threw his injured body in a pickup truck, then shoved him off on the sidewalk in front of the colored hospital and drove away.

Aibileen mentions that she'd like to do some reading. Skeeter tells her to go to the library, but Aibileen reminds her that the library is for whites only. Skeeter offers to check out books and give them to her, and Aibileen quickly suggests a list of twelve books. Aibileen reluctantly admits that she's wanted these books very badly but has been waiting to ask Skeeter about them, because she doesn't know which white rules Skeeter is following; Skeeter replies that she's tired of rules. Skeeter finally finishes typing, and with Aibileen's approval, she sends the manuscript to Elaine Stein.

Skeeter finds that spending time with her white friends has grown more complicated: she notices how condescendingly Hilly speaks to Aibileen, and recalls from Aibileen's stories how harsh Elizabeth Leefolt is to her own child. She still cares about her white friends, but she is even more disturbed about Hilly's separate bathrooms plan after speaking so long with Aibileen.

Aibileen calls her and says that Minny is willing to be interviewed. However, even at the interview, Minny is highly skeptical of the situation; she asks Skeeter why she cares about colored people, and why Skeeter thinks they need her help. Skeeter says that she wants to show the maid's side of things, that perhaps this will change public opinion around issues of race. Minny launches into a story about a very lazy former employer, and then storms out of the room in a rage. Aibileen notes that this was a *good* mood for her.

Chapter 13

(Written from the perspective of Skeeter.) Though Minny often rushes out of the interviews in a rage, she keeps talking to Skeeter about her life story. Minny points out that Skeeter isn't fighting for colored rights, she's just writing about life, and Skeeter concedes that this is true, which angers Minny.

The next day, Skeeter receives an unexpected visitor - Stuart Whitworth. Skeeter is icy to him at first (she asks if he'd like a drink or just a whole bottle of Old Kentucky whiskey), but he apologizes for the way he treated her on their date, even though that was months ago now. He explains that he had been engaged to Patricia van Devender, and this had ended so poorly that he became fearful of new relationships. He likes how Skeeter says exactly what is on her mind, and asks her to go on another date with him. Skeeter refuses at first, then gets in the car with him.

Though they arrive at the restaurant so late that the only thing being served is dessert, Skeeter has a wonderful time. Stuart asks her what she wants out of life, and she replies that she wants to be a writer. He says he hopes that she writes something good, something she believes in. They talk for a long time, and when he finally kisses her, she is overjoyed.

Not long after, Skeeter runs into Susie Pernell, a member of the Junior League, while she's getting books for Aibileen from the library. She stumbles upon a copy of "Compilation of Jim Crow Laws of the South," and she is amazed at their breadth and scope: blacks and whites are not allowed to marry, be buried in the same ground, visit the same barber, or use the same water fountains, movie houses, public restrooms, ballparks, phone booths, and circus shows. She thinks about how these laws are not so different from Hilly's separate bathrooms plan. She puts this book, as well as a book by Frederick Douglass in her bag; she doesn't check them out, because she's afraid that Susie Pernell will talk about her reading "Negro materials."

From the library, she heads to a League meeting, where she is pelted with questions about her burgeoning relationship with Stuart Whitworth (They've been seeing each other for three weeks at this point). Putting down her heavy satchel, which is filled with the stolen books as well as the transcripts of her interviews with Minny and Aibileen, she types the notes for the meeting, but then rushes out early in order to return the car to her mother. When she gets home, she realizes to her horror that she has left her satchel at the League meeting.

Terrified that Hilly will find out about her interviews with the maids, she hops into the car as her mother is driving away. Her mother tells her to get out, saying she has personal errands to run. Skeeter presses her about the nature of see errands, and she replies that they're just routine medical tests, and refuses to answer any more of Skeeter's questions. Though Skeeter is deeply anxious about her health, her mother just tells her to pick her up from the hospital in an hour or so after she gets back from Hilly's.

As soon as Skeeter knocks on Hilly's door, she knows something is wrong. Holly is curt and rude to her, rebuffing Skeeter's friendly attempts to make weekend plans. When Skeeter peers through her satchel, she realizes that her booklet of Jim Crow Laws is gone. Hilly idly points out that Stuart Whitworth's father was active in preventing the integration of Ole Miss. Skeeter leaves the house deeply shaken.

Analysis:

Chapter 11 offers a clear description of Treelore's death: his white co-workers manhandled and abandoned him in front of the colored hospital, not even bothering to bring him inside for treatment. This explains Aibileen's "bitter seed" that grows in response to the racism she sees all around her - her son would probably have lived through his accident if he had been white.

Aibileen's participation in Skeeter's project grows, and she becomes Skeeter's partner in this endeavor. Aibileen's use of her own writing allows her more control over her narrative; she isn't just feeding Skeeter answers, she's directing the conversation as well.

Given the social context, it's possible that the only way for Aibileen to get her story out is to place it on the lips of a white woman. A black woman (especially one who works as a maid and has little formal education) has little chance of publishing a book of her own. Skeeter realizes that Aibileen extremely intelligent and thoughtful, and contributes to Aibileen's budding writing career by getting books for her from the white library; this breaks yet another rule around race, but Skeeter has stopped caring.

After Skeeter finds the book of Jim Crow laws and sees how deeply racism in enshrined in law, she muses about the potential legal consequences of her interviews with the maids. She could be charged with integration violation, or perhaps attacked by vigilantes. A white woman who supports black people will not be tolerated in this charged political climate.

Skeeter's relationship with other white people starts to change on the basis of her new closeness with Aibileen. Looking at her friends through Aibileen's eyes, she starts to see how icy and cruel Elizabeth Leefolt and Hilly are. Skeeter's new perspective on Hilly is confirmed when Hilly goes through her satchel and takes out the Jim Crow laws. Skeeter is terrified that this breach of confidence might have exposed her work with the maids; it's also a sign that Hilly neither trusts nor respects her. Peculiarly, Skeeter has little issue giving Stuart a second chance, which is evidence of the social pressure she is under to get married.

The Help Chapters 14 - 16 Summary and Analysis

Summary:

Chapter 14

(Written from the perspective of Aibileen.) Aibileen is in a tricky position between Skeeter and Minny, continually trying to resolve the arguments between them. The next day, Hilly and her children come over to play with Mae Mobley and Miss Leefolt. While she's playing with the children, Aibileen overhears Hilly mentioning that she read what was in Skeeter's satchel, and that she cannot have colored-supporting friends if her husband William is going to run for office.

Aibileen is terrified. She imagines what will happen if Hilly sees the things that she and Minny have said. Aibileen knows that Hilly will stop at nothing to get revenge. Aibileen could lose her job, her house, her car. Hilly might find a way to send her to jail; she might even target members of Aibileen's family or cause her to become a victim of vigilante justice.

Skeeter calls Aibileen and confesses that she left her satchel with all the interview transcripts and colored-rights materials in it. Aibileen tells her what she overheard Miss Leefolt and Hilly talking about. Skeeter asks Aibileen if she might have heard anything via Yule May, Hilly's maid, but Aibileen says that she hasn't. Skeeter asks if she wants to abandon this plan, but Aibileen replies that if Hilly already know what they're doing, stopping isn't going to save them.

On her way home from work, Aibileen's bus is stopped and everyone is forced off. She sees blue lights flashing in the distance. She walks to Minny's house, and joins Minny and her children listening to the radio. They learn that Medgar Evers, field secretary of the NAACP, was shot and killed in front of his house by a white man. Evers was respected in the Jackson black community for his activism, and his death is a painful blow and a frightening reminder of what can happen to a black person when they try to agitate for change.

Chapter 15

(Written from the perspective of Aibileen.) Still shaken by the murder of Medgar Evers, Aibileen returns to work at the Leefolt household. She tells Mae Mobley a story of two girls (one black and one white) who become friends based on their similarities, ignoring their superficial differences. Mae Mobley loves this story.

Miss Leefolt, Mae Mobley, and Aibileen head to the country club pool and meet up with Hilly and her children. The children play under the watchful eye of Aibileen while the white women chat about upcoming vacation plans. Suddenly, Skeeter appears, coming back from a tennis match. She's happy to see her white friends, but receives a cold reception. She asks if she did something to upset them, and Hilly replies that she found her "paraphernalia," the copy of the Jim Crow laws that Skeeter was carrying around in her bag. Hilly adds that it's pigheaded of Skeeter to think she knows more than politicians, and Skeeter shoots back that Hilly doesn't know anything about politics, her husband probably won't even win the local election. Catching a pleading look from Aibileen, Skeeter softens her tone, apologizing to Hilly and telling her that she's been worried about Hilly's long hours at her husband's campaign. The white women talk for a while, and then Skeeter departs. Both she and Aibileen hope that the Jim Crow laws are all that Hilly read in the satchel.

Chapter 16

(Written from the perspective of Aibileen.) Aibileen's church offers special prayers for the Evers family. But not everyone is content with mere prayer - one young man says that nonviolent action is not enough to keep white people from murdering black people.

Following the service, Aibileen approaches Yule May, Hilly's maid. Once more, she asks Yule May to take part in Skeeter's interviewing project. Yule May says she's afraid to take that risk, having two sons to send to college next year. But she wants to share her awful experiences working for the racist Hilly, and she tells Aibileen she will call her on the phone later.

Analysis:

Chapter 14 reference to real-world events: a specific incident of extreme violence during the Civil Rights era, the murder of Medgar Evers. Evers committed no crime and harmed no one, but he was shot in front of his family because he was the head of the NAACP and an advocate of desegregation. The differing responses to his murder from the white and black communities of Jackson demonstrate how deeply racism is engrained into the social fabric of this time and place. For the white people, this is a way to restore order (or it is something that they are completely unaware of, as in Skeeter's case). For black people, it is an indication that any opposition to the racism of the day can result in violence or murder. This is not lost on Aibileen and Minny, who realize that they are exposing the secrets of white women in their narratives. Evers' murder shows how much is at stake in the fight against racism.

Placing Evers' murder so close to Hilly's discovery of the contents of Skeeter's satchel is a literary method to show exactly what is at stake if Hilly finds out about Skeeter's work with the maids. Aibileen knows that if Hilly has read what she and Minny have said about their work as maids, Hilly will stop at nothing to ruin their lives. She would never tolerate such insolence from a black maid. The women struggle to find out exactly how much Hilly knows without asking her directly, and Skeeter confronts her friend about taking her possessions from the satchel.

The confrontation between Skeeter and Hilly in Chapter 15 highlights the complex nature of friendship. Close friends can wound each other more deeply than archenemies, because they know each other's hopes and fears so well; to wound Hilly, Skeeter undermines her political ambitions for her husband. Skeeter's opinion on Hilly has been irrevocably changed because of her work with the maids, and it remains to be seen if their friendship can survive these changes.

Chapter 14 gives yet another hint that Minny's relationship with her husband is abusive. Previously, Minny has described the fights she has with her husband when he comes home drunk; a few days prior, he shoved her so hard that he bruised her arm. Minny refuses to talk about this aspect of her personal life with Skeeter. The sympathy of a white woman is more embarrassing (or dangerous) than simply enduring her husband's violence.

Chapter 15 and 16 show two different ways that black people cope with racism. Aibileen begins telling stories to Mae Mobley that demonstrate the equality of all people, regardless of color; she hopes that telling these stories to the girl early in life will make her become less bigoted later in life. Aibileen's nonviolent strategy contrasts sharply with the opinion expressed by the young man in Chapter 16 that violence is the only way to make white people stop harming black people. The message of *The Help* sides with Aibileen: stories and compassion, not violence, are the best way to eradicate racism.

The Help Chapters 17 - 18 Summary and Analysis

Summary:

Chapter 17

(Written from the perspective of Minny.) Celia continues to refuse to tell her husband that Minny is working for them - despite the fact that Johnny already knows, and is fine with the situation (though he asked Minny to keep his knowledge a secret). Minny is puzzled by how Celia seems not to understand the rules of white society: she continues to phone Hilly and the other League ladies every day even though they have never replied, and she insists on eating all her meals with Minny.

Minny keeps telling her stories to Skeeter. It is hope for her children's future that leads her to do this. Their father Leroy refuses to have any of them take part in any anti-segregation activities, but he knows nothing about Minny's activities with Skeeter and Aibileen.

Minny finds her work at Celia's house frustrating: Celia often refuses to get out of bed or leave the house, so it's up to Minny to not only finish all of the cooking and cleaning, but to bring in the mail as well. One day, she brings in a small but heavy package that makes a strange sound, as though many tiny glass bottles are clinking together inside it. Celia thanks her and runs off with the package to the empty upstairs of the house, the place where she often mysteriously disappears. Determined to decipher this mystery, Minny decides to investigate the upstairs. Minny sees Celia lying on a bed drinking from a small brown bottle, and Minny assumes that Celia must be drinking large amounts of alcohol. Minny's father was an abusive alcoholic and her husband often drinks too much and hurts her; Minny is infuriated and disgusted that she has yet another alcoholic in her life. Later, Minny sees that the bottles are unlabeled, but "Old Kentucky" (a popular brand of whiskey) is stamped on the glass.

Minny confronts her about this during their cooking lessons, when Celia mentions that they've become friends. Minny says she'd never be a friend of a drunk; she ought to tell Celia's husband about her drinking. Celia bursts into tears and tells Minny that she's fired.

Minny goes to Aibileen's house and tells her what happened, how Celia has been so awful. Aibileen gently reminds Minny of all the employers she's had who have been so much worse than sweet, clueless, lazy Celia, and convinces Minny to go to Celia's house on Monday and ask for her job back.

Chapter 18

(Written from the perspective of Minny.) Celia isn't looking well; she goes into the bathroom while Minny starts cleaning the rest of the house. When Minny gets to the bathroom hours later, she realizes Celia is still inside. Concerned that Celia might have passed out from drunkenness, she opens the door. She sees Celia sitting on the floor near the toilet bowl, which is full of blood. Celia is pale and shaking, and her nightgown is also stained with blood. She asks Minny to get her the phone so she can call her doctor, which Minny does. Minny moves Celia to the bed, though Celia is losing even more blood.

Celia weeps with despair; she was five months pregnant when she had this miscarriage, which is her fourth such. Minny suggests that she shouldn't be drinking whiskey if she wants to stay pregnant. Celia is puzzled at this accusation, and tells Minny that she's been drinking catch-tonic of an Indian make, trying to prevent another miscarriage. Minny is relieved that she isn't an alcoholic. Celia is extremely worried about what her husband Johnny will do. He wants children very badly, but she hasn't been able to bring a pregnancy to term. She's terrified that he will leave her, but Minny assures her that Johnny loves her and would never do such a thing. Suddenly, Celia vomits and starts losing even more blood. Celia passes out from pain and blood loss, and Minny cradles her gently until the doctor comes. Dr. Tate treats Celia, but also claims she's hysterical and tells Minny that she had better not miss her Friday appointment just because she's feeling lazy. Realizing Johnny is about to come home, Minny grabs the cleaning supplies to take care of the blood.

Analysis:

Minny is in a truly peculiar situation: Celia is trying to hide her from Johnny, but Johnny already knows about Minny and is trying to hide this knowledge from Celia. For such a blunt and direct person as Minny, this kind of deception is infuriating, and negatively colors her whole relationship with Celia.

Because of this deception, Minny is quick to look for negative things about Celia. Her clueless kindness infuriates Minny. Her mysterious activities baffle Minny. At last, Minny satisfies her curiosity by finding out what causes her to make frequent trips up into the empty bedrooms upstairs: she's taking swigs from brown-colored bottles. In keeping with her irritation at Celia, Minny assumes the worst: that Celia is an alcoholic.

A frightening incident brings forth Minny's compassion for Celia; Celia has a miscarriage and starts bleeding uncontrollably. Minny takes care of her tenderly and cleans up the blood despite her severe aversion to the substance. Celia's trust for Minny is made clear when she tells the other woman how she has been suffering from miscarriage after miscarriage that she hides from her husband. The brown bottles are "catch tonic," a folk remedy for preventing miscarriage.

This incident brings the two women a little closer. Celia likes Minny a great deal; due to her physical and social isolation (the other white women refuse to talk to her because Hilly hates her), her bond with Minny is the only real friendship in her life.

Minny is not a gentle person and still frequently refers to Celia as a fool, but her gentle actions show her true feelings.

Chapter 17 offers another glimpse at Minny's home life. Her family is not poor or desperate, but their situation is precarious. Minny and her husband, along with their two eldest children, make just enough money to support the family, and they schedule all car rides so that everyone can get to their jobs. For them, the civil rights movement is attractive, but impossible: if Minny, Leroy, or their two oldest children were imprisoned or injured, they would not be able to maintain this delicate balance that is necessary for survival. The white authorities are not the only hazard here: if Minny's small efforts on Skeeter's book are discovered, her husband could react violently.

The Help Chapters 19 - 21 Summary and Analysis

Summary:

Chapter 19

(Written from the perspective of Skeeter.) Sweltering in the July heat, Skeeter continues her work and her relationship with Stuart. She is a bit perturbed when Stuart invites her to go on vacation and stay in the same hotel room as him (unthinkable, since they are not married or even engaged). Though he pressures her, she ultimately refuses. They spend some time together at Skeeter's house, and she asks him the question that has been haunting her: what happened to end his relationship with his ex-girlfriend Patricia? Skeeter wants to know this before she meets Stuart's parents. Stuart refuses to give an answer, saying only that Skeeter would never do what Patricia did. He suddenly gets up and leaves Skeeter's house.

The next day, Pascagoula draws Skeeter aside and tells her that Yule May (who is Pascagoula's cousin) is planning on being interviewed for the book on maids. Skeeter is excited but anxious - she is afraid of what she will learn about the personal life of Hilly Holbrook, who is still her best friend despite their disagreements.

Soon after this, Skeeter receives an unexpected letter from Yule May, who explains that she has been imprisoned for stealing one of Hilly's rings to pay for her twin sons' college tuition. The letter is addressed from the Mississippi State Penitentiary. Skeeter is horrified; she remembers the ring, an ugly, nearly worthless garnet that Hilly never wore. Skeeter learns from Pascagoula that Hilly used her social connections to ensure that Yule May was sentenced to eight times the usual amount of time for petty theft.

Skeeter goes to Aibileen's house, where many prominent members of the Jackson colored community are gathered; she asks what she can do to help Yule May and her family. Aibileen tells her that Yule May had asked Hilly for a small loan of seventy-five dollars to send her boys to college, but Hilly had harshly refused. Now the colored churches are pooling funds to send the two boys to college. Eleven maids come up to Skeeter and tell her that they will help her with the interview project. Skeeter is thankful that this is happening, but heartbroken that it has taken a good woman's imprisonment to make it happen.

During Skeeter's next meeting with Hilly, she can nearly contain her fury at Hilly's version of events; Hilly asserts that black maids often steal family heirlooms so they can sell them to buy liquor pints.

Skeeter and Aibileen start interviewing the maids - eleven have agreed to be a part of the project. She hears stories of tenderness: one maid is concerned about what will happen if she dies before her employer, because the woman is so dependent on her. She also hears stories of horror: one maid's cousin-in-law had her tongue cut out for talking about the KKK. They discuss low pay and hard hours, but also the closeness they feel to some of their charges. Skeeter assures all of them that their names will be kept completely confidential; she also offers each as much money as she can, using earnings from her Miss Myrna column and the allowance her mother gives her. One maid named Gretchen tells Skeeter that she's just trying to make a dollar off black women's stories, and all the maids secretly hate her. Aibileen tells her to leave. Skeeter's next interview is much calmer: a maid named Callie tells her that her employer wrote her a thank-you letter for all the work Callie had done over the years, which Callie appreciated deeply.

Chapter 20

(Written from the perspective of Skeeter.) Stuart's parents warmly receive Skeeter and her family; Stuart himself is still driving back from a business trip. The two sets of parents make conversation; Skeeter's mother mentions that she has heard that the Whitworth's home (a historical landmark) is the centerpiece of historic tours. The Whitworths uneasily admit that Patricia van Deveder's mother is head of the historical council, so they do not take part in historical tours anymore. The group tours the Whitworth home, which is filled with relics of the antebellum- and Confederate-era south, until Stuart returns. The group settles down for dinner. Mr. Whitworth brings up the Life magazine feature on Carl Roberts, a black man who was lynched for saying negative thing about the white Mississippi governor. Skeeter's father says he's ashamed of the violence meted out against black men in the south. Mr. Whitworth says he might agree with the negative things that Carl Roberts said about the governor. Stuart continues to brood over the prior mention of Patricia van Devender.

Mr. Whitworth, extremely drunk, pulls Skeeter aside and asks her if his son is doing all right; he was deeply hurt when Patricia van Devender left him. Skeeter realizes she isn't sure how Stuart really is doing and wonders what she really means to him. She confronts Stuart about what exactly happened between him and Patricia. He confesses that she slept with a Yankee civil rights activist, and that he would not take her back because doing so could jeopardize his father's run for political office. Skeeter asks if he is still in love with Patricia, and Stuart is quiet for a moment before telling her that they should quit things for a while.

Chapter 21

(Written from the perspective of Skeeter.) Skeeter hides her breakup with Stuart from her parents and focuses on typing up the maid interviews. She notices that her mother seems more and more frail: she has grown thinner, she eats little, and she vomits frequently.

Skeeter completes the compilation of interviews, and with Aibileen's help, sends them to Elaine Stein. Skeeter does not know if the book will be published but for the sake of the maids, she hopes that it will be.

After a League meeting, Hilly corners Skeeter and asks her why she has ignored Hilly's instructions to advertise the Home Help Sanitation Initiative in the League newsletter. They argue about the "negro activist materials" (Jim Crow Laws) that Hilly took from Skeeter's bag. Skeeter threatens to report Hilly to the League president, and Hilly says it's no wonder that Stuart left her. Skeeter storms out of the room, and begins to hatch a plan....

Analysis:

If any reader liked Hilly before, they certainly do not anymore. Out of pure spite, Hilly used her connections to make sure that Yule May was imprisoned for years without a fair trial, leaving her family adrift. The ring itself was worthless and Hilly didn't event like it; she mainly likes bulling other people. Hilly seems almost Dickensian in her wickedness.

However, Hilly's cruelty backfires. After the imprisonment of Yule May, an educated and admired member of the black community, the maids of Jackson realize that they have little to lose by discussing their experiences. Skeeter herself is stunned at the cruelty of her former best friend: she knows how little Hilly cared about the ring, and she is even more disgusted at Hilly's refusal to give Yule May a small loan to send her sons to college. Hilly's cruelty toward Yule May marks the end of her relationship with Skeeter as well as a surge of interest in the book about the maids.

Stuart's interactions with Skeeter in chapter 19 are suspicious. He invites her to stay with him overnight in a hotel room (alluding to the possibility of sexual activity), but he does not want to tell her about a major event in his life, the cause of his broken engagement with Patricia. This suggests as sort of shallowness in their relationship: he likes her enough to want to sleep with her, but not enough to tell his secrets to her. His reservation ultimately leads to their breakup.

Gretchen's fierce outburst at Skeeter in Chapter 19 is startling. However, it's true that Skeeter is the one who stands to advance her career most through the publication of this book. She may become a famous writer, but the maids will still be maids (though they may be forty dollars wealthier). Gretchen may be acting out of completely legitimate distrust and anger. By associating opposition to Skeeter's work with such an unlikable character, Kathryn Stockett may be attempting to deflect the criticisms of those who allege that *The Help* makes the stories of black maids secondary to a white woman's ambition.

Chapter 21 expounds upon the theme of the writer's life. Skeeter has put an enormous amount of time and energy into the book about the maids: she has hatched the idea, gained the trust of the maids, conducted interviews with them, typed these interviews, and worked long nights to edit the volume. Despite all of this effort, there is still no guarantee that the manuscript will reach the publishers in time for them to review it, let alone be selected for publication. The writer's life is an enormous amount of effort with very little promise of return.

The Help Chapters 22 - 24 Summary and Analysis

Summary:

Chapter 22

(Written from the perspective of Aibileen.) On Mae Mobley's third birthday, Aibileen wakes her up with a song and a delicious sweets strawberry dessert. (Miss Leefolt is out getting her hair done, as unmindful of her daughter as always.) To Aibileen's surprise, Mae Mobley tells her that she's her real mama, and insists this is true even when Aibileen tries to correct her.

Hilly calls up the Leefolt household in a panic. Miss Leefolt, Aibileen, and Mae Mobley rush to her house, only to find dozens of toilets - of all colors, sizes, ages, and types - sitting on the lawn of Hilly's house. Aibileen pieces the story together listening to Miss Leefolt and Hilly: Skeeter finally printed the information about Hilly's Home Help Sanitation Initiative in the League newsletter, but she made a typo in the piece about the coat drive below it. Rather than asking people to drop off their used coats at Hilly's house, the article invited people to drop off their used toilets.

To make matters worse, it's a slow news week and the toilet debacle finds its way into the pages of newspapers as far distant as the New York Times. This is a funny incident, but it spells social disaster for Skeeter. Hilly and Miss Leefolt kick her out of bridge club and stop speaking to her. Mr. Leefolt tells Aibileen that she'll be fired if he hears about her talking to Skeeter about anything. Aibileen tells Skeeter all about this when she sees her next, and Skeeter tries hard to pretend that none of it matters to her.

Chapter 23

(Written from the perspective of Aibileen.) The civil rights struggle escalates - the march on Washington is a success, but it leads to the bombing of a church. Hilly has several of the lawn toilets installed in people's homes: she calls Skeeter's prank a blessing in disguise. Aibileen tries to positively influence Mae Mobley by telling her stories about the equality of black and white people.

One day, Celia shows up during a meeting of the bridge club, offering her help for the benefit dinner. She receives an icy reception from Hilly, Miss Leefolt, and the their women, but remains undeterred. The other women say they don't need her help, but she buys two tickets to the benefit from them. She offhandedly mentions her maid Minny and how Elizabeth Leefolt (in reality, Aibileen) recommended her. Hilly, who has blacklisted Minny because of their feud, is enraged and determined to get to the bottom of this mystery. Aibileen calls Minny in a panic, telling her that Celia has told Hilly that she hired Minny on Elizabeth's recommendation; this could be disastrous for both women, because Aibileen could get fired and Hilly could have yet another reason to take revenge on Minny.

Chapter 24

(Written from the perspective of Minny.) Luckily for Aibileen and Minny, Hilly eventually decides that Minny must have made up the recommendation, which is a relief because it means Aibileen will not get fired. Minny, however, has other problems to deal with. Her work at Celia's house is made more difficult by a painful cut on her eyebrow; Minny's husband beat her last night, even more savagely than he usually does. Celia notices this injury and tells Minny she must see a doctor. Minny refuses, and Celia tells her to sit down and drink some coffee.

Suddenly, the women catch sight of a deranged naked white man outside the house. He makes threatening gestures at them. Minny and Celia are terrified; they are far out in the countryside, it will take the police far too long to get to the house. When the man smashes a window to get at the women, Minny leaps out to attack him with a broom. The man keeps just out of Minny's reach, shouting taunts at her until she exhausts herself. When she pauses, he strikes her hard, stunning her. Just then, Celia hits the man with a fire poker, exhibiting a strength and fury that Minny did not know she possessed. Celia beats the man until he finally runs away. She explains to the amazed Minny that she used to be a good fighter years ago in Sugar Ditch.

Aibileen comes to see Minny that afternoon, and Minny discusses the events of the day with her. They are both amazed that Celia put herself at risk to defend a black woman. They also try to figure out what to do about Minny's husband Leroy, who is becoming increasingly violent with her.

Celia prepares for the Children's Benefit, which is hosted by the League. Minny delicately tries to explain why the League ladies won't return her calls: she's married to Johnny, Hilly's ex-boyfriend. Celia is oblivious to the social nuances, and assumes that Hilly must think Johnny cheated on her; she decides Hilly should know the truth: that Johnny only took up with Celia after he had broken up with Hilly. Celia puts on a very revealing bright pink dress, and drinks a whole bottle of wine. Minny tries to get her to change into something else or eat something, but Celia ignores her advice. Minny, who will be catering the Benefit, has a very bad feeling about this whole event.

Analysis:

Aibileen continues her mission to instill positive values in Mae Mobley by telling her stories about equality; her own mother rarely talks to her. Aibileen is the one, rather than Mae Mobley's biological mother, who wakes her up with a delicious treat on her birthday. Mae Mobley's insistence that Aibileen is her true mother raises the question: What truly makes a mother? Is it nurturance or is it blood relation? *The Help* seems to suggest that it is nurturance, and someone who is unrelated (and even of a different race) can be an excellent mother.

Hilly, who prides herself on her immaculate public reputation, has her toilet-strewn lawn featured in a number of popular magazines. To make matters worse, it was her friend Skeeter who was behind it all. Hilly's Home Help Sanitation Initiative (which encourages white families to install toilets for the colored help) makes this prank particularly ironic; Hilly is disgusted at the unsanitary nature of toilets, and now her lawn is covered with them. Hilly swiftly takes her revenge by cutting Skeeter off from most social events in Jackson.

Chapter 23 demonstrates the closely entangled nature of social relationships. When Celia shows up at the bridge club and mentions that Minny works for her, she accidentally strikes a powder keg of secrets and deception. Aibileen pretended to be Miss Leefolt recommending Minny; Aibileen is desperate to hide this from the white women, and Miss Leefolt wants to clear her name with Hilly, who hates Minny and would never recommend her to anyone. Hilly wants to make sure that Minny never tells anyone (especially someone she dislikes as much as Celia) about the Terrible Awful. Minny is dismayed that Hilly now knows where she is working. With this small, innocent act, Celia has complicated a number of social relationships.

The events in Chapter 24 demonstrate that Celia is not as simple or helpless as she seemed before. Her ferocious defense of Minny opens up a new window to her character: as a child, she was a tough fighter in Sugar Ditch, but she has largely left behind that part of her personality in order to move up in society as Johnny Foote's wife. Minny develops a newfound respect for Celia; she notes that the other woman is somewhat like herself, someone who takes no shit. This incident also demonstrates how much Celia cares for Minny. She could have saved herself by running inside and leaving Minny to the mercy of the naked man, but instead she decided to put herself in danger to help her friend.

The Help Chapter 25 Summary and Analysis

Chapter 25

It is the night of the Jackson Junior League Annual Ball and Benefit, the most important social event of the year. The cream of white society is present, as well as a number of black servants (including Aibileen and Minny). The women of the League (Hilly, Elizabeth Leefolt, and even Skeeter, who has become a social outcast) are dressed in elegant and conservative styles that show very little skin.

Celia Foote, wearing a tight and revealing pink dress, arrives with her husband Johnny Foote. Her attire is completely inappropriate for this solemn occasion, and prompts staring from the men and disapproval from the women. Celia has a number of alcoholic beverages and is quite oblivious to her faux pas. She is determined to find Hilly and explain to her that Johnny did not cheat on her with Celia.

The guests are all seated, and Hilly begins her speech, thanking all in attendance for their contributions to the Benefit. The silent auction starts. When Celia is in the bathroom Hilly sidles up to Johnny and flirts with him; Johnny is disgusted and brushes her away. He tells Celia nothing of this, and Celia has a few more strong drinks.

The winners of the silent auction are announced: one of the winners is Hilly, who will take home a chocolate custard pie made by Minny. Hilly, however, is absolutely furious - she is sure this must be a terrible prank of some sort, because she did not bid on the pie and she still hates Minny because of the "Terrible Awful." Minny is equally shocked at this announcement.

A rather drunk Celia takes advantage of Hilly's state of shock to chat with her. Hilly tries to leave, but Celia grabs her cuff and accidentally rips it. Hilly accuses Celia of trying to blackmail her way into the League by signing Hilly's name on the pie, but Celia is puzzled about this and tries to explain her relationship with Johnny. There is an unfortunate silence in the room when Celia loudly informs Hilly that she got pregnant from Johnny after he and Hilly had broken up, and the entire room hears this sensitive statement. Celia vomits in the middle of the room.

After the Benefit is over, Hilly discovers that it was her own mother, Miss Walters, who signed Hilly up for the pie. Miss Walters says that she will never be able to forget the thing that happened with Hilly and Minny's pie. What exactly was that? The readers still have yet to find out....

Analysis:

The portrayal of Celia as the strong protector of her friend in the previous chapter encourages the reader to relate to her, which makes the intensely embarrassing situation at the Benefit even more impactful. Celia wears inappropriate clothing, gets unacceptably drunk, shouts about her out-of-wedlock pregnancy, rips Hilly's dress, and vomits on the ground. Because of the reader's sympathy for Celia, this situation reflects more negatively on the stringent social rules of the Benefit than on Celia herself, who is just trying to conduct herself in an unfriendly environment.

Chapter 25 also raises the mystery of the pie. Hilly is furious at being signed up to win Minny's pie at the silent auction. Though Minny is well known for her delicious treats, Hilly is certain that only someone who wants to humiliate her would sign her up for the pie. She initially blames the drunk Celia, who is so startled by Hilly's antagonism that she vomits. It later becomes clear that Hilly's own mother signed her up for the pie, as a way of playing a joke on her daughter. Still, the reader is left with the question: what pie-related incident happened to Hilly?

This chapter is unique in being the only one in the entire book written in the third person. The effect is a more omnipotent narration, one that gives the reader the chance to experience the thoughts of all the characters. Rather than focusing on developing a character through descriptions of what she sees and hears, the author can instead focus on the event. This offers a "birds' eye view" of the event, honing in on events and images that none of the three narrators would be likely to notice or comment on. This writing method also draws the reader's attention to this chapter as a significant one, a turning point in the narrative.

The vernacular style of this chapter most resembles Skeeter' sections: it uses American Standard English, and does not employ the dialect that characterizes the speech of Minny and Aibileen. This raises a number of uncomfortable questions: why is this manner of narration used as a neutral standard, when it in fact differs from most of the writing in the book?

The Help Chapter 26 - 28 Summary and Analysis

Summary:

Chapter 26

(Written from the perspective of Minny.) Johnny Foote calls Minny the day after the Benefit and asks her to check in on his wife Celia (he is away on a planned trip to a hunting camp). Celia just lies in bed for three full days, refusing to move or touch any food. She tells Minny that she should have stayed where she belonged, and Johnny should have married properly; she doesn't understand why Hilly was so furious at the pie, and why she assumed Celia was the one who signed her up for it. Celia decides that she's going to leave Johnny and move back to Sugar Ditch.

Minny, who feels very guilty that Celia is so worried about the pie, decides to tell Celia her deepest secret. She explains that after Hilly spread rumors about her being a thief, Minny baked some of her own feces into a chocolate custard pie and fed Hilly two slices of it before telling her what was in it. Hilly was furious, but terrified to be known in Jackson as the woman who ate a black woman's feces. Minny explains to Celia that Hilly must have thought she knew about the story, and that's why she was so vicious to her. Minny encourages Celia not to leave her husband, because then Hilly will have beaten them both.

The next day, Celia leaves her bed and eats some food. Despite the cold and the rain, she goes outside and chops down the mimosa tree. Hilly notices a check that Celia has written to reimburse Hilly for ripping her dress - the check is made out to "Two-Slice Hilly."

Chapter 27

(Written from the perspective of Skeeter.) Skeeter calls Elaine Stein to check in about the manuscript, which she plans to send it in January. Elaine tells her that this is not acceptable; Skeeter is a completely unknown writer and if she is to have any chance at all of getting her book noticed, she needs to have it in before December 21st. Elaine also tells Skeeter that she needs to interview her own childhood maid Constantine for the book. Skeeter is shocked to realize she will only have nineteen days to finish writing two more interviews, but she is determined to see this project through.

Skeeter has been completely outcast from the League. Hilly was furious about the toilets on her law and asked Skeeter how long she had been planning to humiliate her like this. When Skeeter could not find a satisfactory answer, Hilly stopped speaking to her; it has been well over four months since the two women last spoke. Skeeter tried to remain friends with Elizabeth Leefolt, but Elizabeth also stopped speaking to her. This social humiliation is compounded when Hilly publicly replaces her as the editor of the League newsletter.

One night, Skeeter comes home from a long drive to find Stuart Whitworth on her porch. He explains that he drove to San Francisco to confront Patricia, and that he's resolved any lingering feelings that he has for her. He wants to start things with Skeeter again, but Skeeter feels as though she has already given him too many chances.

She pours herself into typing up the last few stories, realizing she has even less time than she originally thought because of the time it will take to mail the material to New York City. At Aibileen's suggestion, she decides to call the book *Help.* Aibileen also agrees to tell her what happened to Constantine.

Stuart Whitworth continues to stop by her house, often exchanging only a few words with Skeeter. One day he stops by as her mother is on the porch, shivering under blankets despite the warm air. Skeeter expects her mother to rebuke her for being so unfriendly to a potential husband, but her mother tells her that Stuart is not worthy of her.

Aibileen writes Skeeter a letter telling her what happened to Constantine. Skeeter learns that Constantine's daughter Lulabelle was extremely light-skinned, which made it impossible for her to live in segregated Mississippi: she looked white but she was actually black, and was treated harshly by both communities. To make matters worse, Constantine got pregnant out of wedlock. Constantine gave her up to an orphanage in Chicago because she needed to keep working for Skeeter's family. Lulabelle got back in contact with Constantine a couple years ago, and came to visit her in Mississippi. Lulabelle came to a society function that Skeeter's mother was hosting, and she helped herself to all the treats meant for the white guests. When Skeeter's mother confronted her about this unacceptable behavior, Lulabelle mocked her and then spat in her face in front of all the guests. Skeeter's mother told Constantine that Lulabelle could never show her face in Mississippi again. Lulabelle said that Skeeter's mother couldn't keep them apart, not after Constantine had been forced to give her up after her father's death. Skeeter's mother knew this was a lie and told Lulabelle so, saying that her father had run off the day she was born and that Constantine didn't want her because she was so light-skinned.

Constantine moved up to Chicago with her daughter and died three weeks later. Skeeter confronts her mother about this, who asserts that she could not tolerate this kind of rudeness, but she did not know that Constantine would leave and pass away. Skeeter is heart-broken and angry, but she cannot bring herself to be too harsh on her frail mother.

Skeeter, Aibileen, and Minny put the last touches on their manuscript. They are very concerned that people in Jackson will figure out whom the book is about, and the identities of the black maids who told their stories. Minny decides that they could use some "insurance," and she suggests putting the Terrible Awful in the book, because then Hilly (who would be most likely to discover the truth) would make sure that no one else figured out whom the book was about. It is also risky, because this move could ensure that Hilly knows exactly whom the book is by and about, possibly bringing down her wrath on the women who wrote it. Ultimately, the three women decide that Hilly's shame at the Terrible Awful is greater than her desire for revenge, and they add it to the book. Skeeter sends out the final version only a few days before the deadline, unsure if it will reach its destination on time.

Chapter 28

(Written from the perspective of Skeeter.) The family doctor reveals to Skeeter that her mother has stomach cancer, and has only a few weeks to live. Skeeter is devastated, but she does her best to make her mother comfortable at home. Despite her pain and weakness, Skeeter's mother remains determined, writing lists of unflattering clothes that Skeeter should not wear and making years' worth of future hair appointments for her daughter.

Stuart continues to visit Skeeter despite her coldness toward him. One night he presents her with a ring and asks her to marry him. Skeeter is stunned; she does love Stuart, and she also wants to give her mother the happiness of seeing her daughter engaged. But she decides that if they are going to be married, he has to know about the book she has written with the maids. After she tells him this, Stuart takes back the ring and leaves.

Elaine Stein tells Skeeter that they have decided to publish her book. The advance will only be a few hundred dollars and the first printing will be small, but Skeeter, Aibileen, and Minny are delighted at the news. Their joy is dampened, however, by the fear that the white women of Jackson might recognize themselves and take their revenge on the maids.

Analysis:

At last, the "Terrible Awful," the reason for the continuing hatred between Minny and Hilly, is revealed. The racist Hilly has eaten two pieces of a pastry containing a black woman's feces. Hilly has built a great deal of her public reputation on the idea that black people are so dirty that they require separate bathrooms, so this incident would tarnish her reputation beyond all repair. The timing of this story is significant: Minny tells this story to Celia to assuage her humiliation at the events of the Benefit and to prevent her from leaving her husband, signifying how close the two women have become.

Celia's act of chopping down the mimosa tree in chapter 26 marks a major turning point for her. She hates this tree and has often wished it was removed, but leaves it up for the sake of appearances. By chopping it down, Celia symbolically chooses her own integrity and interests over pleasing other people. She won't pretend to like the mimosa tree anymore, and she also won't pretend to like Celia and her friends.

The sad incident between Constantine's daughter Lulabelle and the Phelan family show how racism can still destroy a close relationship built over decades. By pretending to be white, helping herself to food, speaking rudely, and spitting in Skeeter's mother's face, Lulabelle offered an insult that could not be ignored. Rather than just firing Constantine, however, Skeeter's mother did something even crueler: she exposed the gentle lie that Constantine had told her daughter about why she had given her up. This act also alienated Constantine from the Phelan family, and she did not have time to resolve this argument because of her untimely death.

Despite these cruel acts toward Constantine and her daughter, Skeeter's mother grows more sympathetic. A doctor reveals to Skeeter that she is terribly sick with stomach cancer, which explains her insisting that her daughter settle down and marry. Skeeter's mother also supports her daughter during Stuart's unwelcome return; she tells her daughter not to cheapen herself by taking him back. Despite her flaws, Skeeter's mother wants a happy life for her daughter.

Skeeter finds herself completely socially outcast. Hilly and Elizabeth refuse to speak to her, and Hilly kicks her out of the League. Her only relationship in the white community is with Stuart, who is trying to win her back. When Stuart asks her to marry him, Skeeter exhibits her tendency for brutal honesty by telling him about her work with the maids, knowing that she cannot start a life with him if she hides this crucial piece of information. He cannot handle this revelation, and he leaves with the ring.

The Help Chapter 29 - 31 Summary and Analysis

Summary:

Chapter 29

(Written from the perspective of Aibileen.) Despite the heat and hard work at the Leefolt household, Aibileen carries a secret joy - the book about the maids has been published. The book is entitled *Help,* and Skeeter has given a copy of the book to each of the maids who were interviewed for it. The cover is light blue, with a peace dove on it, and "Anonymous" is listed as the author. Copies of it appear in Jackson bookstores and libraries. Aibileen waits with bated breath to see if Miss Leefolt will purchase the book, but so far it has no appeared in the house.

Aibileen's church holds a quiet celebration. The reverend tells her that the community understands the need for secrecy, but they want to recognize her incredible achievement. The church gives her a copy of *Help* signed by nearly every member of the black community in Jackson, and they also give her one to pass on to Skeeter, thanking her for all her work. Aibileen weeps for joy, happy that the two years of work has finally come to fruition.

One day while Aibileen is working in the Leefolt household, a book review program comes on the television. The book they're reviewing? *Help*, of course! Miss Leefolt starts watching because the reviewer was a member of her college sorority; the reviewer calls the book trash, and tells the ladies of Jackson not to spend their husbands' hard-earned money on it. Miss Leefolt misinterprets this to mean that the book is about Jackson, and she heads out to buy herself a copy. Aibileen watches these developments with trepidation, unsure if Miss Leefolt will realize that part of the book is about her.

Chapter 30

(Written from the perspective of Minny.) Minny is furious that the book review show has led to rumors that the book is about Jackson. Though she knows Celia (who has energetically taken up gardening) would never fire her, she is afraid of what Hilly will do. Her worry intensifies when Aibileen tells her that Miss Leefolt bought a copy for Hilly.

Celia learns from her doctor that she will never be able to carry a pregnancy to term. She also tells her husband Johnny how Minny saved her when she had the miscarriage, and Johnny thanks Minny profusely. He holds Celia and asks her never to leave him. Minny, who is heavy with yet another pregnancy, weeps with Johnny and Celia.

At home, Minny's husband asks her what she's up to, and wrenches her arm despite her pregnancy. Minny is afraid to tell him about the book, because she knows it will prompt him to be even more violent with her.

Chapter 31

(Written from the perspective of Aibileen.) Aibileen overhears the bridge clubwomen discussing *Help*; they agree that it must be about Jackson, and they wonder if they've met the black maids who narrate the book. Hilly grins wickedly and says she's determined to find out the identities of everyone in the book. Miss Leefolt, however, reads right past her chapter; she likely does not recognize herself in the portrayal of the woman who does not know how to love her own child.

Aibileen stops by the grocery store to buy a snack for Mae Mobley, and overhears two white women talking about *Help*. They whisper about Aibileen to each other, saying that they bet that's her. Her only hope is that Hilly will read about the Terrible Awful and shut down all of these rumors.

Analysis:

Skeeter, Aibileen, and Minny have reached the final portion of the writer's struggle: their book has been published, and their efforts were not in vain. Still, the unexpected success of the book raises the danger that some people will recognize people or events depicted in it, which could put the maids in danger.

The televised book review demonstrates how easily rumors can be started. The reviewer suggests that the book could be about anywhere, even Jackson; Miss Leefolt interprets this to mean that the book is definitely about Jackson. The review also sparks conversation among other women about the identities of the people depicted in the book. In some cases, people are so narcissistic that they are unable to recognize themselves in the unfavorable portrayals offered by the maids, such as Miss Leefolt. However, as Aibileen discovers when she overhears the conversation in the store, other people in the community are putting the pieces together.

Chapter 30 compares two very different types of love. Celia is devastated to find out that she is infertile, but Johnny says he will always love her and begs her not to leave him. They love each other deeply, and their minor deceptions are their ways of trying to prove their own worth to each other. In contrast, the relationship between Minny and her husband Leroy shows the darker side of love. Usually Leroy does not hit Minny when she's pregnant (Aibileen thinks this is one of the reasons why Minny has so many children), but he notices how anxious she is about the publication of the book and hurts her because she won't tell him what she has been doing. This is a frightening and unhealthy relationship dynamic.

The Help Chapters 32 - 34 Summary and Analysis

Summary:

Chapter 32

(Written from the perspective of Minny.) Aibileen tells Minny that Hilly is telling white women to fire their maids because of *Help*, but she isn't guessing correctly. One maid has already been fired, and Hilly is pressuring another of her friends to send her maid to jail for talking about her secrets. The sudden appearance of Leroy interrupts the conversation, and Minny runs back in her house.

Late at night, a very drunk Leroy asks Minny what her big secret is. She refuses to tell him, and knows that it is only the child in her belly that saves her from a terrible beating. She cannot cope with Leroy's increasing violence; despite her tough talk, she is terrified to fight back against her husband. The only thing that could make this worse is if Leroy found out that she was part of the book about the maids.

As she goes to sleep one night, Minny is certain that she hears a scream come from the direction of Hilly's house.

Chapter 33

(Written from the perspective of Skeeter.) Woken by a scream, Skeeter lies awake reflecting on her life. She's panicked that the women of Jackson have correctly discerned that the book is about their community, and she is worried about what will happen to the maids. She desperately wants to leave Mississippi, where she no longer has any friends. She has been applying for jobs outside of Jackson, but she also does not want to abandon Aibileen in the middle of this mess.

While out on an errand to get medicine for her mother, Skeeter runs into Elizabeth Leefolt and Lou Anne Templeton. After Elizabeth leaves, Lou Anne tells Skeeter that Hilly is spreading rumors that it was Skeeter who wrote the book about the maids. Hilly is also demanding that Lou Anne fire her maid Louvenia, who took part in the interviews for the book. Lou Anne says she could never fire Louvenia, who has supported her throughout her depression and suicide attempts. Lou Anne tells Skeeter that she is grateful for what Louvenia said about her in the book, and that if Hilly tells her to fire Louvenia again, Lou Anne will tell Hilly to her face that she deserved that pie. Skeeter is horrified by this - the pie story, the "Terrible Awful," is supposed to be their insurance to keep Hilly quiet. Lou Anne says she isn't even entirely sure the story is about Hilly, and in fact she heard Hilly saying that the book really wasn't about Jackson at all. In any case, Lou Anne offers her support to Skeeter. Skeeter leaves, stunned in two counts: that Hilly may have discovered their secret, and that Lou Anne Templeton is so much stronger than she ever knew.

One night, Skeeter receives a letter from a New York City address. She has no time to open it, because Hilly drives up in the darkness, looking disheveled and saying that she is going to sue Skeeter for what she put in her book. Skeeter feigns ignorance, but Hilly tells her that she will destroy her and the black maids as well, specifically naming Aibileen and Minny. Skeeter's mother, whose health has improved greatly, cuts short the confrontation. After Hilly storms off, Skeeter calls Aibileen immediately and tells her about Hilly's threat; Aibileen says there's nothing to do but wait and see what happens. Skeeter also tells them that she has received a job offer from Harper's magazine in New York City. Aibileen congratulates her, but Skeeter doesn't want to abandon her. Minny fiercely tells her that there is nothing at all left for her in Jackson, and that she better get her white butt to New York City. Skeeter makes her decision: she will go to New York.

Chapter 34

(Written from the perspective of Aibileen.) *Help* is still the talk of the town. Hilly is now shrilly insisting that the book isn't about Jackson at all, but a number of white women have recognized the stories that are about them.

Aibileen chats with Minny, who tells her one of the happiest stories to come out of the situation: one maid's boss sat down with her and asked how she could be a better employer, and she really listened to what the maid said. Still, Minny is jumpy and anxious. Aibileen realizes what a profound sacrifice she made by putting the pie story in the book - she did it to protect the other maids, but she also put herself in danger.

Mr. Leefolt catches Mae Mobley and her little brother Ross pretending to be anti-segregation activists sitting at Woolworth's. Aibileen taught them this game through the secret stories she tells the children, but Mae Mobley lies to protect her and says it was her racist teacher Miss Taylor who taught her this game.

Hilly drops her silverware off at Miss Leefolt's house for Aibileen to clean, and she returns them to Hilly's house the next day. Skeeter comes to the door of Aibileen's home that night, telling her that the publishing company is going to print five thousand more copies of *Help* due to high demand, and the all of the maids who were interviewed for the book will be getting at least one hundred more dollars. Skeeter also tells Aibileen that she is going to be the next Miss Myrna; Skeeter told her boss at the newspaper that she had been getting the answers from Aibileen all along, and he agreed to hire Aibileen to write the column (as long as she doesn't tell anyone that she is colored). Skeeter says goodbye, because this is the last time she will see Aibileen before heading to New York.

Early in the morning, Aibileen receives a frantic call from Minny. Minny's husband has been fired from his job on the orders of William Holbrook, Hilly's husband. He tried to kill Minny, locking her in the bathroom and threatening to set the house on fire. She escaped with her children to a gas station, and is going to stay in the country with her sister for a little while. Aibileen tells Minny that she has to leave her abusive husband: she has a solid job with Celia and Johnny, and she will be getting another lump sum of money from the book. Minny decides to leave her violent husband.

When Aibileen arrives at work, Hilly and Miss Leefolt confront her. Hilly says that several pieces of her silver were missing after Aibileen cleaned them, and threatens to press charges. Hilly also tells Aibileen that Miss Leefolt is going to fire her for this. When Miss Leefolt leaves the room to check on her children, Hilly hisses that she will never forgive Aibileen for the things that she wrote about Elizabeth Leefolt in her book. Aibileen threatens to send letters to everyone in Jackson if she is sent to jail for her theft, telling them all about Hilly's incident with Minny's pie. Hilly abandons her plan to send Aibileen to jail, but still demands that Miss Leefolt fire her.

Aibileen says goodbye to Mae Mobley, who is crying loudly. She reminds Mae Mobley that she is a kind, smart, important girl. Then she leaves, parted forever from the little girl.

Walking away from the house, Aibileen also realizes how free she is. She will have a little money coming in from the book and the Miss Myrna column. She thinks about continuing to write what she has seen, about starting over and making a new life for herself.

Analysis:

The book about the maids has impacted racial relationships in a number of ways. In some cases, the book has had the dreaded effect of exacerbating racism; one woman fires her maid on Hilly's orders because of what she read in the book. But in other cases, the book results in a more equitable relationship between black and white women. One white woman starts to treat her maid better because she doesn't want her secrets to get out; another white woman sits down with her maid and has a true conversation with her for the first time ever.

The "insurance" that Minny added to the book (a recounting of the Terrible Awful) has the desired effect of forcing Hilly to publicly deny that the book was about Jackson. However, the women don't realize that because of Hilly's position of racial and economic privilege, she can take revenge without explaining her reasons. She uses her husband's connections to get Minny's husband fired from his job; he doesn't know exactly why he was fired but he knows his wife had something to do with it, so he attempts to kill her before she decides to leave him forever, and head to her sister's house. Hilly frames Aibileen for the minor theft of some silverware, and forces Miss Leefolt to fire her.

The separation of Aibileen and Mae Mobley is a cruel one, almost like separating a mother and daughter. Aibileen is concerned about how she will make a living, but she is even more concerned about what will happen to Mae Mobley without her. Will she become a racist? Will she internalize her mother's cruelty and neglect? Aibileen imagines a strong, powerful, adult Mae Mobley, who remembers all of the lessons that Aibileen taught her, and who respects herself and others.

All three of the main characters (Skeeter, Minny, and Aibileen) are poised on the edge of a great change in their lives. Skeeter's new beginning is a bit more promising than that of the others; though she cannot publicly claim credit for the book about the maids, her connections with Elaine Stein have earned her a position at Harper's Magazine in New York City. Because of her secure job at Celia's house, Minny has left her abusive husband after his threat to murder her; however, it is not clear how she will support her five children without his assistance. Aibileen was been fired from the Leefolt household, but she has a steady income from the book and the Miss Myrna column, and she realizes that she is free to do what she wants with her life.

The three main characters have been freed of the things that trapped them. In Skeeter's case, this was Mississippi society; in Minny's, her violent husband; in Aibileen's, her difficult job at the Leefolt home. On the other hand, Hilly is trapped by the same social conventions she once participated in it. As Aibileen wisely notes, she will be in a prison of her own making for the rest of her life, forever trying to convince people that she didn't eat the pie.

The Help Symbols, Allegory and Motifs

Bathrooms (Motif)

Bathrooms are one of the recurring motifs in the novel. This begins with Hilly's Home Help Sanitation Initiative, which requires all white families to have a second bathroom for the use of their black maids. This policy creates a number of difficulties for Aibileen and other maids, and prompts Skeeter to start her work on the book about black maids.

The bathroom motif highlights the down-to-earth focus of the novel; everyone uses bathrooms every day, but few of us think very much about it. In the same way, the novel focuses on the daily lives of maids rather than major historical actors.

The history of the period informs this motif: segregated bathrooms and public facilities were major sites of contestation during the Civil Rights movements.

Aibileen's Bitter Seed (Symbol)

After the tragic death of her son Treelore, Aibileen says, "A bitter seed was planted inside a me. And I just didn't feel so accepting anymore" (pg. 3). Later on, when Miss Leefolt gleefully tells her about the home's new segregated bathrooms, and Aibileen notes "I [...] feel that bitter seed grow in my chest, the one planted after Treelore died (pg. 14).

Treelore's death destabilized Aibileen's life, and affected her views on all matters of justice. Though it began with her son's death, this bitterness eventually grew in response to the many other types of injustice and tragedy that Aibileen faces every day. This sense of justice is particular attuned to racial inequalities; Aibileen feels the seed grow after Miss Leefolt tells Mae Mobley that Aibileen is dirty and diseased. As Aibileen assists Skeeter with the book about the maids, she stops mentioning her bitter seed. This symbol is an example of the way that personal suffering can grow into a desire to prevent the pain of others.

Celia's Mimosa Tree (Symbol)

Celia despises the mimosa tree that stands outside her house, and early in the novel she often stares at it with an axe in her hand. It is only after the disaster at the Benefit that Celia chops down the mimosa tree during a rainstorm.

Chopping down the mimosa tree symbolizes the control that Celia takes over her own life. Celia hates the tree and finds it ugly, but she leaves it up for appearance's sake. In a similar way, she tries to ingratiate herself to Jackson society by smoothing over the rough edges in her own personality. In both cases, Celia is more concerned with what other people think than with her own opinions.

After the Benefit, she realizes that Hilly will always hate her and Jackson society will never accept her. There is no longer any reason to keep up such appearances, so she chops down the ugly tree. Rather than being a victim of her circumstances, she takes control and removes what she hates from her life.

Pies (Motif)

Minny is famous for her great skill at cooking, and particularly for her delicious pies. The recurring motif of pies shows the significance of household chores in the novel, as well as the services rendered to white households by the black maids. But the "Terrible Awful," as well as the stories that the maids put into the book, indicate that shocking things might be hidden in sweet and homey treats.

The Dove

Featured on the cover of the book written by Skeeter and the maids, the dove is described in the book as "a sign of better times to come" (pg. 462). It connects the book with the progressive elements of the sixties, which focused on peace and equality. It also demonstrates how the book itself is a messenger of peace, meant to bridge the great divide between black and white women.

The Help Metaphors and Similes

"If chocolate was a sound, it would've been Constantine's voice singing. If singing was a color, it would've been the color of that chocolate" (pg. 78) (Metaphor)

This metaphor that Skeeter uses when recalling Constantine's singing shows the mutually reinforced connections between music, color (the brown color of Constantine's skin), and the sweetness of chocolate. It vividly depicts the deep, lovely quality of Constantine's voice.

"She like one a them baby chickens that get confused and follow the ducks around instead" (pg. 106) (Simile)

Aibileen describes Mae Mobley this way when she notices that she is more affectionate with the colored help than with her own mother. The simile highlights Mae's attachment to Aibileen, which is as odd as a baby chicken following around a duck. It also emphasizes Mae's young and vulnerable nature by comparing her to a helpless baby animal.

"And there be Miss Skeeter in a red dress and red shoes, setting on my front steps like a bullhorn" (pg. 118) (Simile)

This quote references the bright colors Skeeter is wearing on her tall frame, but also emphasizes that her appearance on Aibileen's doorstep is as unexpected as a loud noise.

"[Her] smile is a fat child's at the Seale-Lily Ice Cream window. The button on her red suit coat bulges" (pg. 206) (Metaphor)

Hilly is planning a double date with Skeeter and Stuart. Peculiarly, she seems most interested in getting her husband William to spend time with Stuart, which may be related to the fact that William is running for office and Stuart comes from an influential family. When Skeeter agrees to this double date, Hilly says "Good," and her smile is described as a fat child's (p. 206).

Hilly is clearly no child - she rules the Junior League with an iron first, and she manages every aspect of social life among white women in Jackson. However, she is often self-centered, and lacks an understanding of the needs and feelings of others. Like a child at an ice cream shop, she thinks only of ways to satisfy her own desires.

"[She] says her family pattern is Chantilly, but she'll be picking out her own new pattern when she gets married. 'Since I consider myself an independent thinker and all.' Carlton pets her on the head and she nudges against his hand like a cat. They both look up and smile" (pg. 134) (Simile)

Shortly before she rushes out to her first, ill-fated date with Stuart, Skeeter meets her brother's girlfriend, whom she refers to as Ponytail Girl. She describes her in the above way, a self-proclaimed independent thinker.

By comparing Carlton's girlfriend to a cat, this simile emphasizes the dehumanizing nature of white southern femininity. She might consider herself an independent thinker, but the only real choice she has is between the patterns on her silverware. Even this small exercise in choice is only significant as a way to make her boyfriend's family like her.

"Mississippi is like my mother. I am allowed to complain about her all I want, but God help the person who raises an ill word about

her around me, unless she is their mother too" (pg. 528) (Simile)

Author Kathryn Stockett writes this in her epilogue to *The Help.* Whenever remarks to Stockett about the loveliness of her state, she points out the violence in its history. Whenever someone comments on how awful Mississippi is, she points outs its beauty. Despite how dear the state is to her, she recognizes that it is not perfect. In this way, Mississippi is comparable to a parent.

The Help Irony

The Bitter Irony of Racism

The hypocritical nature of racial segregation is a primary focus of the novel. It is odd to believe that black people are able to clean homes and watch over children, but are not fit to use the same bathroom facilities as whites. This bitter irony is not lost on Aibileen, who says, "I use my colored bathroom from now on. And then I go on and Clorox the white bathroom again real good" (pg. 14).

The poor starving African children

At the same time that she is pushing a policy to have separate bathrooms for the colored help, Hilly spearheads a fundraising initiative in order to benefit the "Poor Starving Children of Africa"; Skeeter notes, "I wait for Hilly to catch the irony of this, that she'll send money to colored people overseas, but not across town" (pg. 331).

Children on a faraway continent are worthy subjects for charity, but African-American children right down the road are not worthy of attention. Likewise, it's an honorable thing to raise a little money, but it's unacceptable to change the social structures that cause such suffering. Part of this is due to the fact that charity allows one to feel superior to those whom one is helping, whereas to participate in social activism one must relate to others who are in very different circumstances.

The Toilets in Hilly's Lawn

Skeeter is angry after her argument with Hilly, who found "Negro activist materials" in Skeeter's purse. Hilly demands that Skeeter print the information about the Home Help Sanitation Initiative in the League newsletter, something that Skeeter has been putting off for months. Skeeter does so... but she makes a little change that has big consequences. She puts the notice about the Home Help Sanitation Initiative right next to an ad about a coat drive, but rather than asking members to drop off their old coats at Hilly's address, Skeeter asks them to drop off their old toilets.

Hilly comes home from a weekend trip to find over thirty old toilets in her yard, a sight so marvelous that it is featured in the New York Times. For a woman who has maintained that toilets used by colored people carry diseases, this is a difficult and ironic situation.

Skeeter having toilets installed for the help

Hilly declares the toilet debacle a blessing in disguise when she has them installed in white homes for the use of the help. Sadly, Skeeter ends up aiding in a cause that she meant to undermine.

The Help Imagery

"In fact, the shades of brown on Constantine were endless. Her elbows were absolutely black, with a dry white dust on them in winter. The skin on her arms and neck and face was a dark ebony. The palms of her hands were orangey-tan and that made me wonder if the soles of her feet were too, but I never saw her barefooted" (pg. 76)

Recalling her close childhood relationship with her family's maid Constantine, Skeeter describes Constantine's skin in this way.

Stockett deftly uses a number of different shades to describe Constantine's appearance. In addition to conveying a vivid picture, this description of Constantine's many colors may also undermine the rigid black-white binary. If so many colors are contained within just one person, it's absurd that society should set up boundaries between people of different colors.

"On either side of me, the cotton fields are a glaring green, fat with bolls. Daddy lost the back fields to the rain last month, but the majority bloomed unharmed. The leaves are just starting to spot brown with defoliant and I can still smell the sour chemical in the air" (pg. 83)

This is a vivid description of the beautiful scenery of the south. It is also noteworthy for its use of unique adjectives to convey the appearance of the fields. Rather than being covered in bolls, the fields are "fat" with bolls; instead of being covered with brown spots, the leaves are "starting to spot brown."

"We step out onto the blacktop, feel the heat cover us. I got the paper sack in one hand, Mae Mobley's hand in the other and we trudge across the steaming black lot. Gridlines make it like we on a charcoal grill, roasting like corncobs. My face getting tight, burning in the sun. Baby Girl lagging back on my hand and looking stunned like she just got slapped. Miss Leefolt panting and frowning at the door, still twenty yards away, wondering, I reckon, why she park so far. The part in my hair get to burning, then itching, but I can't scratch at it cause both hands is full, then shoo! somebody blow out the flame. The lobby's dark, cool, heaven" (pg. 237)

Stockett uses a number of strategies to convey the experience of walking in the heat. She uses similes that draw on cooking to convey the feeling of walking on blacktop in extreme heat. She describes the reactions of the other characters, not mentioning how sweaty or hot they are, but instead describing how Mae Mobley is "stunned" by the heat, and how Miss Leefolt "frowns" at the faraway door. She also describes a minor but uncomfortable sensation in the narrator's own body - the way that heat and sweat can contribute to an itchy scalp.

"In the lounge, the air seems to still. Husbands drinking their whiskeys stop in mid-sip, spotting this pink thing at the door. It takes a second for the image to register. They stare, but don't see, not yet. But as it

turns real - real skin, real cleavage, perhaps not-so-real blond hair - their faces slowly light up. They all seem to be thinking the same thing - Finally.... But then, feeling the fingernails of their wives, also staring, digging into their arms, their foreheads wrinkle. Their eyes hint remorse, as marriages are scorned (she never lets me do anything fun), youth is remembered (why didn't I go to California that summer?), first loves are recalled (Roxanne...) All of this happens in a span of about five seconds and then it is over and they are just left staring" (pg. 379)

This quote vividly captures the appearance of Celia, clad in a scandalously skimpy tight pink dress, at the conservative Benefit. This use of imagery is effective because it does not linger on descriptions of Celia, but rather on the reactions that she inspires among the men in the room. This allows the reader to fill in the details of Celia's appearance from her/his own imagination.

The Help Civil Rights

The Help is shaped by the struggles of the Civil Rights movement. The end of the Civil War in 1865 abolished slavery in the United States. However, the southern states introduced a number of laws that kept black people in inferior positions: black people and white people were not allowed to use the same libraries, bathroom, water fountains, schools, theaters, train cars, or other public facilities. This separation was referred to as segregation.

Moreover, black people were forbidden from living in certain areas and working at lucrative jobs. Black people who fought against these rules were often subject to vigilante violence by groups such as the Ku Klux Klan; this violence was rarely prosecuted in any court of law.

In 1954, the landmark legal case Brown vs. the Board of Education of Topeka led to the end of "separate but equal" laws; the Supreme Court ruled that the establishment of separate public schools for black and white students violated the Constitution. This legal decision paved the way for integration, leading to a number of challenges to similar legislation over the next decade. The 1960s saw a number of efforts to desegregate universities and restaurants; these efforts were met with intense and often violent backlash, but were ultimately successful.

The Help Literary Elements

Genre

Historical fiction

Setting and Context

Jackson, Mississippi, early 1960s

Narrator and Point of View

The novel uses rotating narration: Aibileen, Minny, and Skeeter take turns describing the events of the book in the first person. This allows us to see the same scene through very different eyes, which is useful in creating a well-rounded narrative since Minny and Aibileen have different experiences than Skeeter due to their race. This also allows the reader to sympathize with each of the main characters equally.

Tone and Mood

Even when the novel is dealing with serious issues, the tone generally remains light; the tone does not become melodramatic or tragic. This is made clear through the numerous humorous comments made throughout the book. For example, after Aibileen thanks Minny for her courage in contributing to the book about the maid, "[Minny] roll her eyes and stick out her tongue like I handed her a plate a dog biscuits. 'I knew you was getting senile,' she say.'" Even in this serious time, the author keeps the tone humorous.

Protagonist and Antagonist

The three narrators (Aibileen, Minny, and Skeeter) are the protagonists. Hilly is the primary antagonist.

Major Conflict

The overarching conflict is that of human beings versus social norms - more specifically, versus racism and sexism. Each of the primary characters brings a distinct set of conflicts. Aibileen is trying to cope with her son's untimely death, support Mae Mobley despite her mother's neglectful ways, and deal with the oppressive social norms for people of color in her community. Minny is trying to hold down a job so that she can provide for her family, and find ways to deal with the violence committed against her by her husband; later, she tries to unravel the mystery of Celia's life.

Climax

The climax occurs when "Help" is finally published; the consequent conclusion of the plot is the various characters and Jackson at large dealing with the fallout from the publication.

Foreshadowing

In the early parts of the novel, Minny makes frequent reference to the "Terrible Awful" that she did to Hilly. On page 53, shortly after she starts working for Celia Foote, Minny worries that Hilly will try to have her fired for "the Terrible Awful Thing" she did. Later, Minny refuses to make a chocolate pie for Celia, promising herself that she will never make one again after Hilly (pg. 146). This foreshadows the moment after the Benefit when Minny finally reveals to Celia that she baked her own feces into a pie and fed it to Hilly.

Understatement

N/A

Allusions

The book alludes to the real-life vigilante violence perpetuated against black people by organizations such as the Ku Klux Klan. In describing her fears about the consequences for writing the book about the maid, Aibileen describes the following scenario: "[...] That knock on the door, late at night. That there are white men out there hungry to hear about a colored person crossing whites, ready with they wooden bats, matchsticks. Any little thing'll do" (pg. 224).

Imagery

N/A

Paradox

Minny includes the "Terrible Awful" in her narrative as a type of insurance, a way to protect the other women. Hilly will likely recognize the events and people described in the book and plot revenge against the maids, but she will also be motivated to hide the fact that the book is about Jackson so that people do not realize she was the one to eat the feces pie. Hilly is caught in a paradox, torn between her desire to harm those who offend her and her wish to keep the Terrible Awful a secret.

Parallelism

The differing reactions of the white and black population to the murder of Medgar Evers show parallels. The black population is terrified about this outbreak of violence against a deeply respected member of their community; this is illustrated by Minny's horrified comment to Aibileen: "'Things ain't ever going to change in this town, Aibileen. We living in hell, we trapped. Our kids is trapped'" (pg. 230). The white establishment, on the other hand, sees the vigilante murder of Evers as simply returning things to business as usual. On the radio, the white mayor of Jackson publicly refuses President Kennedy's directive to put together a biracial commission. "'Jackson, Mississippi, is the closest place to heaven there is,' he say. "And it's going to be like that for the rest of our lives'" (pg. 231). These comments are united by the comment sentiment that nothing will change in Jackson Mississippi. For white people, this constitutes a heavenly existence, but for black people this means trying to survive in hell.

Metonymy and Synecdoche

The title of the book ("The Help") is an example of metonymy. "The help" is a term for the black maids who perform work for white households; one of their attributes is used to signify their whole person. This particular attribute references the services they render to white households, which demonstrates the subordinate role of the black maids - they are valuable only for "the help" that they offer white women.

Personification

While Minny cleans Celia's home, she takes special care to clean a giant taxidermied bear, and imagines that this object is glaring at her. "I dust the shelves in the hunting room, vacuum the bear while he stares at me like I'm a snack. 'Just you and me today,' I tell him" (pg. 159). This demonstrates Minny's feeling that she is constantly being watched as she goes about her work.

The Help Links

Her family hired me as a maid for 12 years but then she stole my life and made it a Disney movie

http://www.dailymail.co.uk/femail/article-2033369/Her-family-hired-maid-12-years-stole-life-Disney-movie.html

Information about the lawsuit brought against Kathryn Stockett.

Association of Black Women Historians on "The Help"

http://www.abwh.org/images/pdf/TheHelp-Statement.pdf

Detailed critique of *The Help* from an academic black women's association.

This Life: Kathryn Stockett on her childhood in the Deep South

http://www.dailymail.co.uk/home/you/article-1199603/This-Life-Kathryn-Stockett-childhood-Deep-South.html

Stockett's reflection on her childhood.

The Civil Rights Movement

http://www.history.com/topics/black-history/civil-rights-movement

A short history of the civil rights movement.

The Help Essay Questions

1. ***The Help* is very critical of the organized racial segregation of the 1960s, but some people have alleged that this novel perpetuates a subtler version of racism. They argue that the novel highlights the ungrammatical speech of the black maids, and makes their story secondary to that of a white woman (Skeeter). Do you think this claim has merit? Why or why not?**

   I think this claim does have merit. At the end of the novel, Skeeter lands a prestigious job in New York City on the basis of the book she wrote about the maids, but the maids themselves find their circumstances unchanged. Minny's husband has been fired from his job on the basis of her work on the book, and she must leave her family before her husband kills her. Aibileen is fired from her job with the Leefolts due to Hilly's interference. Skeeter and the maids did not benefit equally from the publication of the book. In the same way, the author Kathryn Stockett may have benefited financially and professionally from exploiting the stories of the maids in her own life.

2. **The novel takes place nearly a century after the end of slavery, yet many of the black characters in the book still work extremely demanding and unpleasant jobs. What factors (social, economic, educational, etc.) keep them in these sorts of positions?**

   Aibileen mentions that her mother was a maid and her grandmother was a house-slave. She also says that her mother pulled her out of school in order for her to start work as a maid, because she needed to support the family. Aibileen's parents were not paid a great deal for their work (perhaps because they are black), so their daughter must leave her education in order to contribute to the family. Without education, she cannot move to another job. Additionally, if Aibileen tried to leave her job as a maid for another position, she might be subject to harassment for being "uppity"; we see evidence of this in Hilly's treatment of Yule May, who is one of the most educated maids in Jackson.

3. **The novel depicts very warm relationships between black maids and the white children they care for - Aibileen and Mae Mobley, Constantine and Skeeter. However, these relationships are also marred by racial and economic inequality. Can there be genuine affection in such a complicated and unequal relationship? Can you compare the relationships depicted in this book with your own experiences of caregiving?**

   I think there can be genuine affection in such a complicated and unequal relationship. After all, an adult must have some tender feelings for the child, or else he or she would just quit the job. Aibileen mentions that she has become a specialist at raising children, which shows that she chooses this line of work because she likes it. Her relationship with Mae Mobley is similar to my experiences babysitting for a local family. Some people might think that just because I was being paid for this work means that I didn't really care for the child, but in fact I worked even harder at this job because I cared so much for the child.

4. **Why does Skeeter give Stuart a second chance after their first date was so disastrous? Do you think this was her own choice, or was she pressured to do this? Would you have made the same choice that she did?**

   I think Skeeter was under some pressure from her mother, Hilly, and society to give Stuart a second chance. Skeeter's mother was constantly asking why she did not have a steady boyfriend, and Hilly wanted Skeeter to date Stuart in order to further her own husband's political career. Skeeter was also the only one in her friend group who was not yet married, so she was probably more likely to give Stuart a second chance than another woman in a similar situation. I would not have made the same choice as Skeeter, because I believe that Stuart ruined his first impression by being drunk and rude during their first date. Behaving in such a way during a first meeting is not a sign of good things to come.

5. ***The Help* is often praised for its well-rounded, complex characters. How does the author create such characters, and what sorts of literary strategies does she use? Focus your analysis on one character.**

   I will look at the character of Minny. To create a unique voice for Minny, the author uses a form of African-American vernacular when writing from her perspective, which differentiates her from Skeeter and other white characters. Unlike the other narrators, Minny frequently makes sarcastic and funny remarks. For example, when she gets the job with Celia, she notes, "Relief hits me. [...] I don't have to move to the North Pole. Won't Santy Claus be disappointed" (pg. 45). Minny is also very reluctant to bring up aspects of her personal life; it is very late in the book when she mentions how violently her husband acts towards her. This gives the reader the impression of a person who likes to keep certain things to herself.

6. **Chapter 25 is the only chapter in the book that is written in the third person. Why do you think the author chose to do this? What does it accomplish? Does this chapter have a different tone than the other chapters?**

   I think the author chose to do this in order to show the scene from a neutral perspective. If she wrote it from the point of view of one of the narrators, that narrator would add her own opinions and perspective to it. For example, if Aibileen or Minny wrote it, they would focus on the catering work they were doing rather than on the events unfolding. Likewise, if Skeeter narrated it, she might hone in on the exclusion she felt from the other members of the League, and may not have paid much attention to what was happening with Celia.

7. **Many of the main characters in *The Help* are social outsiders; for example, Skeeter is considered something of a misfit for being more interested in writing than boys. However, in other places and times such behavior would be considered normal. How much of a person's character is shaped by the time period in which he or she lives?**

   I think a great deal of a person's character is shaped by the time that she or he lives it. It is possible that some personality traits are inherent and would hold true anywhere, but those traits will be perceived differently in various societies. For example, Minny's sharp tongue might have made her a famous comedian if she had been born today; but in 1960s Jackson, her acerbic wit is just a liability. The cold reception she receives makes her more bitter and angry, which in turn makes her say harsher things.

8. **Choose one historical event mentioned in the novel (The assassination of Medgar Evers, the march on Washington, the invention of the birth control pill, the war in Vietnam, etc.) and research it. What was the impact of this event on society at the time? How did people react to it? How do the reactions of the characters in *The Help* compare to the reactions of real people?**

   The invention of the birth control pill was hailed as a revolution for many women, despite the fact that it was initially prescribed only for married women. Like many people, Skeeter marveled at this incredible new technological development. There were a number of religiously based objections to this medicine when it was introduced, but this historic development is not reflected in *The Help*. Minny does not make mention of the birth control pill, but it could have changed her life by allowing her to limit the size of her family.

9. **There are many instances of revenge in the book - Skeeter's prank with the toilets, Hilly's imprisonment of Yule May, Minny's "Terrible Awful," the way Hilly ostracizes Celia. Which is one example of revenge that goes too far, and what is one example of revenge that you think is justified? Why?**

   I think that the bid that Miss Walters placed on the pie at the Benefit is an example of revenge that is justified. By placing the bid, she reminded her daughter of the "Terrible Awful," but did so in a way that would not be apparent to anyone who did not know the story. Miss Walters was angry with her daughter for placing her in a retirement home, and this was a clever way to remind her that Miss Walters knew her darkest secret. One example of revenge that went too far was Skeeter's prank with the toilets on Hilly's lawn. Though this was a humorous scene, Skeeter should have known that it would have major consequences.

10. **The women of *The Help* deal with a variety of problems related to sex/gender and sexism, but their experiences differ due to race, class, and age. Choose two characters from the novel and compare the types of sexism that they struggle with.**

    Skeeter struggles with demands that she marry and give up her professional ambitions. She wants to keep working, but her family and her friends would rather she settle down. On the other hand, Minny was married at a young age and is forced to continue working as a maid to support her family; unlike Skeeter, Minny does not struggle to work outside of the home.

The Help Quizzes

1. **What is the name of Aibileen's dead son?**
    A. Terrance
    B. Treelore
    C. Trevor
    D. Tyrone

2. **What does Hilly call her crusade to create separate bathrooms for the help?**
    A. Home Help Sanitation Initiative
    B. Clean Home Crusade
    C. Black Bathroom Initiative
    D. Separate Bathrooms Measure

3. **What does Aibileen write every night?**
    A. Part of her novel
    B. Her prayers
    C. A journal entry
    D. Conversations she has had that day

4. **Where did Celia Foote grow up?**
    A. Sugarloaf
    B. Mud Ditch
    C. Sugar Hill
    D. Sugar Ditch

5. **What does Celia ask Minny to teach her?**
    A. How to apply makeup
    B. Cooking
    C. Flower arranging
    D. How to clean silver

6. **What was the only job that Skeeter applied to during her senior year?**
    A. Editor
    B. Salesgirl
    C. Clerk
    D. Stenographer

7. **What is Elaine Stein's position at Harper & Row publishers?**
    A. CEO
    B. Senior editor
    C. President
    D. Hiring manager

8. **Where is Skeeter's first job out of college?**
    A. Jackson Journal
    B. Mobile Monthly
    C. Birmingham Beacon
    D. Harper & Row

9. **What kind of compensation does Skeeter offer Aibileen for her help with the Miss Myrna column?**
    A. Five dollars per article
    B. A medal
    C. Protection from Hilly's harassment
    D. A typewriter

10. **Why doesn't Skeeter tell her mother about her date with Stuart?**
    A. Her mother dislikes Stuart's family
    B. Stuart is black
    C. Her mother wants her to marry someone else
    D. Her mother will become too involved

11. **During her first interview with Skeeter, what's the question that catches Aibileen off guard?**
    A. What do you dislike about your job?
    B. Do you hate having separate bathrooms?
    C. Have you ever thought that you were smarter than your white boss?
    D. Do you think the violence against civil rights protestors is justified?

12. **What does Aibileen's note to Skeeter say?**
    A. I know how to make the teapot stop rattling
    B. I know why the caged bird sings
    C. I know why bowls are round
    D. I know why mayonnaise removes bathtub stains

13. **What document in Skeeter's satchel does Hilly read?**
    A. Her interviews with Aibileen
    B. A copy of the Jim Crow laws
    C. Her interviews with Minny
    D. Her diary

14. **The assassination of what major figures terrifies Minny and Aibileen?**
    A. Bayard Rustin
    B. Medgar Evers
    C. Martin Luther King, Jr.
    D. Nina Simone

15. **What crisis does Minny help Celia survive?**
    A. Abandonment by her husband
    B. The mimosa tree falling on her house
    C. A miscarriage
    D. A kitchen injury

16. **What is one of Hilly's only redeeming qualities?**
    A. Her love of animals
    B. Her love for her children
    C. Her charity towards the help
    D. Her excellent cooking

17. **What qualities best describe the character of Aibileen?**
    A. Warm and wise
    B. Inquisitive and shy
    C. Imperious and rude
    D. Sharp-tongued and tough

18. **What qualities best describe the character of Minny?**
    A. Imperious and rude
    B. Inquisitive and shy
    C. Sharp-tongued and tough
    D. Warm and wise

19. **What qualities best describe the character of Skeeter?**
    A. Imperious and rude
    B. Sharp-tongued and tough
    C. Warm and wise
    D. Literary-minded and shy

20. **What is Yule May imprisoned for?**
    A. Taking seventy-five dollars from Hilly's wallet
    B. Striking one of Hilly's children
    C. Telling Hilly that she's a fat racist with the morals of a streetwalker
    D. Stealing one of Hilly's rings (one she doesn't even like)

21. **What convinces the rest of the maids to take part in Skeeter's project?**
    A. The murder of Medgar Evars
    B. Yule May's imprisonment for stealing Hilly's ring
    C. The money Skeeter offers them
    D. The attack on Louvenia's grandson

22. **What is one of the books that Aibileen asks Skeeter to get from the white library?**

A. A book by Audre Lorde
B. Harry Potter and the Sorcerer's Stone
C. A book by Abraham Lincoln
D. A book by Freud

23. **What do the Jim Crow Laws attempt to prevent?**

A. Illiteracy
B. Theft
C. Social mingling of black and white people
D. Drunk driving

24. **What best describes Skeeter's opinion of Hilly's separate bathrooms initiative?**

A. She thinks it will prevent disease
B. She thinks it will pose difficulties in toilet training white children
C. She thinks it's similar to the Jim Crow Laws
D. She thinks it will protect black maids from harassment by white men

25. **What does Minny discover in the upper rooms of Celia's house?**

A. A dead baby
B. A dollhouse
C. A phone that Celia uses to call women in the Junior League
D. Brown bottles that appear to contain alcohol

Quiz 1 Answer Key

1. **(B)** Treelore
2. **(A)** Home Help Sanitation Initiative
3. **(B)** Her prayers
4. **(D)** Sugar Ditch
5. **(B)** Cooking
6. **(A)** Editor
7. **(B)** Senior editor
8. **(A)** Jackson Journal
9. **(A)** Five dollars per article
10. **(D)** Her mother will become too involved
11. **(A)** What do you dislike about your job?
12. **(A)** I know how to make the teapot stop rattling
13. **(B)** A copy of the Jim Crow laws
14. **(B)** Medgar Evers
15. **(C)** A miscarriage
16. **(B)** Her love for her children
17. **(A)** Warm and wise
18. **(C)** Sharp-tongued and tough
19. **(D)** Literary-minded and shy
20. **(D)** Stealing one of Hilly's rings (one she doesn't even like)
21. **(B)** Yule May's imprisonment for stealing Hilly's ring
22. **(D)** A book by Freud
23. **(C)** Social mingling of black and white people
24. **(C)** She thinks it's similar to the Jim Crow Laws
25. **(D)** Brown bottles that appear to contain alcohol

The Help Quizzes

1. **Why does Minny stop working for Mrs. Walters?**
    A. Mrs. Walters dislikes Minny's food
    B. Mrs. Walters becomes tired of Minny's sharp tongue
    C. Hilly sees Minny using Mrs. Walters' bathroom
    D. Hilly sends Mrs. Walters to a retirement home

2. **What college did Skeeter graduate from?**
    A. Vanderbilt
    B. Arkansas State
    C. Ole Miss
    D. Tuskegee

3. **What does Miss Leefolt build in her house?**
    A. A model airplane
    B. A separate bathroom for the colored help
    C. A second bedroom
    D. A den

4. **How did Johnny Foote react when he discovered Minny was working in his house?**
    A. He drove her off his property and told her never to return
    B. He laughed and welcomed her
    C. He tried to kill her with an axe
    D. He had her arrested

5. **What type of tree grows outside Celia's house? (hint: she hates it)**
    A. Mimosa
    B. Birch
    C. Yew
    D. Willow

6. **At the end of their ill-fated date, what does Stuart say to Skeeter?**
    A. He doesn't like uppity women
    B. He wants to sleep with her
    C. He vomits on her shoes
    D. He wasn't ready for a date

7. **How does Aibileen keep the teapot from rattling?**
    A. By putting a towel under the teapot
    B. By writing down her memoirs and reading them to Skeeter
    C. She is not able to do this
    D. By taking her time

8. **What does Elaine Stein think of Aibileen and Skeeter's interview?**

A. She dislikes it, and tells Skeeter she should focus on writing fiction

B. She never replies to Skeeter

C. She likes it, but isn't sure how Skeeter will get more maids to talk to her in this political climate

D. She likes it, but tells Skeeter she wants to work with Aibileen instead

9. **What shocking thing does Skeeter discover in a copy of Frederick Douglass, American slave?**

A. It was checked out by Constantine

B. Frederick Douglass is an ancestor of Aibileen

C. It was never checked out by anybody

D. Someone has scrawled a racial epithet in it

10. **What group of people does Hilly (ironically) choose as the subject of the League's charity project?**

A. The poor starving children of Africa

B. The gays

C. African-Americans in North Carolina

D. The poor starving children of China

11. **How does Hilly obtain Skeeter's satchel?**

A. Skeeter accidentally leaves it at a League meeting

B. Skeeter accidentally leaves it at Hilly's house

C. Hilly takes it from Skeeter when she isn't paying attention

D. Skeeter lets her borrow it, but forgets to take the important papers out

12. **Why does Stuart come to Skeeter's house after their ill-fated first date?**

A. To ask her to write for his father's campaign

B. To tell her exactly what happened between him and Patricia van Devender

C. To compliment her writing

D. To apologize and ask her on a second date

13. **What of her children does Minny think most takes after her?**

A. Kindra

B. Treelore

C. Leroy

D. Sugar

14. **What is an example of the actions that the Jim Crow Laws prohibit?**
A. The use of the same restroom by blacks and whites
B. The unlicensed killing of crows
C. Driving tractors on city streets
D. Selling liquor on Sundays

15. **What happens to Yule May's sons after their mother is imprisoned?**
A. They move out of Mississippi
B. They both take jobs spreading tar
C. The colored churches raise money for them to both attend college
D. They take out student loans to go to college

16. **What does Celia do when the naked man attacks Minny?**
A. Hides until the man goes away
B. Stabs him
C. Beats him with a fire poker
D. Runs away

17. **What is shocking about Gretchen's interview with Skeeter?**
A. Gretchen tells Skeeter about the sexual abuse she suffered from her employer
B. Gretchen tells Skeeter about seeing a young gay boy viciously beaten by his father
C. Gretchen tells Skeeter that Hilly had Yule May imprisoned
D. Gretchen tells Skeeter that the maids secretly hate her and are lying to her

18. **Which of the following is NOT one of the embarrassing things that Celia did at the Benefit?**
A. Vomited in public
B. Spoke loudly about getting pregnant from Johnny
C. Wore a very revealing dress
D. Slapped Hilly

19. **What is Hilly shocked to find on her front lawn?**
A. A sign support school integration
B. A horse head
C. Dozens of toilets
D. A flock of pink flamingoes

20. **What unforgivable thing does Hilly say to Skeeter?**
A. She's read her interviews with Aibileen and Minny
B. Skeeter's mother is dying
C. She isn't surprised that Stuart dumped her
D. She's a bad writer

21. **What was the unforgivable thing that Patricia van Devender did to Stuart?**

A. She slept with a Yankee civil rights activist
B. She slept with a colored man
C. She left him for a woman
D. She told Stuart she didn't want to marry him

22. **Who placed a bid on Minny's pie in Hilly's name?**

A. Minny
B. Celia
C. Skeeter
D. Her mother, Miss Walter

23. **What makes the Whitworth home special?**

A. The Whitworths bought it from Skeeter's relatives
B. It is haunted
C. It is built to look like a Roman villa
D. It is a historic landmark

24. **What terrible thing does Minny's husband do to her?**

A. Spends all her money
B. Burns all of her possessions
C. Cheats on her with a woman named Coco
D. He beats her

25. **What kinds of stories does Aibileen tell Mae Mobley?**

A. Stories about racial equality
B. Tales about loving mothers
C. Traditional African-American folktales
D. Hans Christian Andersen fairy tales

Quiz 2 Answer Key

1. **(D)** Hilly sends Mrs. Walters to a retirement home
2. **(C)** Ole Miss
3. **(B)** A separate bathroom for the colored help
4. **(B)** He laughed and welcomed her
5. **(A)** Mimosa
6. **(D)** He wasn't ready for a date
7. **(B)** By writing down her memoirs and reading them to Skeeter
8. **(C)** She likes it, but isn't sure how Skeeter will get more maids to talk to her in this political climate
9. **(D)** Someone has scrawled a racial epithet in it
10. **(A)** The poor starving children of Africa
11. **(A)** Skeeter accidentally leaves it at a League meeting
12. **(D)** To apologize and ask her on a second date
13. **(A)** Kindra
14. **(A)** The use of the same restroom by blacks and whites
15. **(C)** The colored churches raise money for them to both attend college
16. **(C)** Beats him with a fire poker
17. **(D)** Gretchen tells Skeeter that the maids secretly hate her and are lying to her
18. **(D)** Slapped Hilly
19. **(C)** Dozens of toilets
20. **(C)** She isn't surprised that Stuart dumped her
21. **(A)** She slept with a Yankee civil rights activist
22. **(D)** Her mother, Miss Walter
23. **(D)** It is a historic landmark
24. **(D)** He beats her
25. **(A)** Stories about racial equality

The Help Quizzes

1. **What does Skeeter's mother think is the most important thing to get out of college?**
   A. A job
   B. A diploma
   C. Good grades
   D. A husband

2. **Where does Skeeter's mother say Constantine went?**
   A. New Orleans
   B. Chicago
   C. Detroit
   D. Little Rock

3. **What is Minny's greatest skill as a maid?**
   A. Cooking
   B. Cleaning
   C. Washing silver
   D. Childcare

4. **Who sets up Stuart and Skeeter on a date?**
   A. Aibileen
   B. Hilly
   C. Skeeter's mother
   D. Elizabeth Leefolt

5. **What is the only chapter of the book written in the third person?**
   A. Chapter 2
   B. Chapter 26
   C. Chapter 13
   D. Chapter 25

6. **What is the "Terrible Awful"?**
   A. Miss Walters placed Hilly's name in a bid for one of Minny's pies
   B. Celia vomits on Hilly
   C. Minny baked some of her own feces in a pie she fed to Hilly
   D. Minny stole some of Hilly's silverware

7. **What does Celia do after the disastrous Benefit?**
   A. Moves to Sugar Ditch
   B. Send Hilly a check for four thousand dollars
   C. Pretends nothing is wrong
   D. Says she should leave Johnny

8. **What event prompts Minny to tell Celia about the "Terrible Awful"?**

A. Celia's defense of Minny against the crazed naked man
B. Celia's misery after the disastrous Benefit
C. Minny's desire to embarrass Celia
D. Celia's miscarriage

9. **What makes Skeeter's mother tell her not to cheapen herself?**

A. Stuart Whitworth begging her to take him back
B. Wearing ill-fitting clothes
C. Talking to a strange man
D. Writing the maid's stories

10. **Who are the ironic beneficiaries of the Jackson Junior League Annual Ball and Benefit?**

A. The African-American community in Detroit
B. The poor starving children of China
C. The poor starving children of Africa
D. Minny's family

11. **What was one of the reasons Constantine gave up her daughter?**

A. Constantine was raped, and her daughter looked too much like her rapist
B. Constantine did not like her daughter
C. Giving her to the white orphanage offered her a chance at a better life
D. Her daughter was light-skinned and could not live in segregated Mississippi

12. **What was NOT one of the things that Lulabelle did at the Phelan household?**

A. Mocked Mrs. Phelan for utilizing colored help but barring colored guests
B. Tried to sign up for an all-white organization
C. Baked her feces into a pie that she fed to Mrs. Phelan
D. Spat in Mrs. Phelan's face

13. **Why didn't Constantine write Skeeter back?**

A. She died three weeks after she moved to Chicago
B. Mrs. Phelan forbade her to contact the family
C. Lulabelle wouldn't let her
D. Constantine hated the Phelan family so much for what they did to her daughter

14. **What animal is on the published version of Help, the book that Skeeter wrote about black maids?**
   A. A panther
   B. A dove
   C. A sparrow
   D. A mockingbird

15. **Who finally tells Skeeter what happened with Constantine?**
   A. Mr. Phelan
   B. Pascagoula
   C. Aibileen
   D. Hilly

16. **What is the "insurance" that the women add to the book about maids?**
   A. Lullabelle's treatment of Skeeter's family
   B. The "Terrible Awful" that Minny did to Hilly
   C. A terrible secret about every family in Jackson
   D. Details about Hilly's sex life

17. **What prompts the white women of Jackson to think that Help might be about them?**
   A. Hilly's discovery of Skeeter's interview notes
   B. A comment from one of their maids
   C. Hilly
   D. A book review on TV

18. **Why did Constantine tell her daughter that she had to give her up?**
   A. The Phelan family made her do it
   B. She was sick and her husband had died
   C. They were too poor to feed her
   D. She was an unmarried mother

19. **Who tells Lulabelle the truth about why Constantine put her up for adoption?**
   A. Pascagoula
   B. Hilly
   C. Constantine
   D. Skeeter's mother

20. **What does Hilly do when she finds out that the pie story is in Help?**
   A. She tells everyone that Minny is a liar
   B. She sends Skeeter to jail
   C. She bakes feces into a pie that she serves at a League function
   D. She tells everyone that the book isn't really about Jackson

21. **What is the important message that Aibileen tries to instill in Mae Mobley?**

A. That black people are superior to white people
B. That she is beautiful
C. That her mother is an idiot
D. That she is smart, kind, and important

22. **What does Lou Anne Templeton say about her relationship with her maid Louvenia?**

A. She hates Louvenia, but cannot fire her because then everyone will know the book is about them
B. She thinks Louvenia slept with her husband
C. Louvenia is the reason she gets out of bed
D. She hid in a trunk with Louvenia when Union soldiers marched through Jackson

23. **How does Skeeter's mother react when Skeeter tells her about writing the Miss Myrna column**

A. Skeeter has never cleaned anything in her life
B. She tells her to find another job that will exercise her creative writing skills
C. She congratulates her for obtaining this job
D. She says nothing

24. **Why does Celia want to keep Minny a secret from her husband?**

A. Celia is afraid that her husband will beat her
B. Celia wants to hide her spending habits from her husband
C. Celia wants her husband to think she is a good housekeeper
D. Celia knows her husband hates black people

25. **How does Aibileen manage to convince Celia that Miss Leefolt recommended Minny?**

A. She tells Celia about the Terrible Awful
B. She imitates the voice of Miss Leefolt
C. She tells Celia that Miss Leefolt asked her not to tell about Minny because Minny is a thief
D. She tells Celia that Miss Leefolt asked her not to tell about Minny because all her friends want to hire her

Quiz 3 Answer Key

1. **(D)** A husband
2. **(B)** Chicago
3. **(A)** Cooking
4. **(B)** Hilly
5. **(D)** Chapter 25
6. **(C)** Minny baked some of her own feces in a pie she fed to Hilly
7. **(D)** Says she should leave Johnny
8. **(B)** Celia's misery after the disastrous Benefit
9. **(A)** Stuart Whitworth begging her to take him back
10. **(C)** The poor starving children of Africa
11. **(D)** Her daughter was light-skinned and could not live in segregated Mississippi
12. **(C)** Baked her feces into a pie that she fed to Mrs. Phelan
13. **(A)** She died three weeks after she moved to Chicago
14. **(B)** A dove
15. **(C)** Aibileen
16. **(B)** The "Terrible Awful" that Minny did to Hilly
17. **(D)** A book review on TV
18. **(B)** She was sick and her husband had died
19. **(D)** Skeeter's mother
20. **(D)** She tells everyone that the book isn't really about Jackson
21. **(D)** That she is smart, kind, and important
22. **(C)** Louvenia is the reason she gets out of bed
23. **(A)** Skeeter has never cleaned anything in her life
24. **(C)** Celia wants her husband to think she is a good housekeeper
25. **(D)** She tells Celia that Miss Leefolt asked her not to tell about Minny because all her friends want to hire her

The Help Quizzes

1. **What's the name of Minny's husband?**
   A. Leroy
   B. Oliver
   C. Lawrence
   D. Larry

2. **How many children does Minny have?**
   A. Two
   B. Five
   C. Six
   D. Three

3. **Who is the first maid to be interviewed by Skeeter?**
   A. Aibileen
   B. Yule May
   C. Minny
   D. Constantine

4. **What is the most important thing that Minny must remind herself while working for Celia?**
   A. Don't be tempted to steal silverware
   B. Make sure everything is extremely clean
   C. Stay out of her business
   D. Don't backtalk

5. **How does Skeeter orchestrate the toilet prank?**
   A. Skeeter puts the toilets there
   B. Skeeter makes a "mistake" in the League newsletter asking people to drop off their used toilets
   C. Skeeter encourages all the people who hate Hilly to bring a toilet
   D. Skeeter asks Aibileen and Minny to help their friends bring the toilets

6. **What do most of the maids do with the money that Skeeter offers the for working on the book?**
   A. Tithe it to the church
   B. Contribute it to the college fund for Yule May's sons
   C. Invest it in their own children's education
   D. Spend it on household expenses

7. **What is NOT one of the mixed emotions that Aibileen, Minny, and Skeeter feel upon learning that the book about the maids will be published?**

    A. Sorrow that Aibileen will lose her job
    B. Fear of retribution
    C. Joy that people will read their work
    D. Dismay that the first printing run is so small

8. **What revelation prompts Stuart to call off his engagement with Skeeter?**

    A. He learns that Skeeter's mother is dying
    B. He learns about Skeeter's falling out with Hilly
    C. Patricia tells him that she still loves him
    D. Skeeter tells him about the book she is writing with the maids

9. **What do Skeeter, Aibileen, and Minny decide to call their book about the maids?**

    A. Help
    B. Colored Maids of the South and the Families for Whom They Work
    C. Black Beauty
    D. Maid in Heaven

10. **What event prompts Celia to chop down the mimosa tree?**

    A. The Benefit
    B. Telling Johnny about Minny
    C. Fighting off the naked crazy man
    D. Her fourth miscarriage

11. **What are Skeeter's plans at the end of the book?**

    A. To take over her family's farm
    B. To live in Chicago
    C. To travel the world and write stories
    D. To move to New York City and work for Harper's Magazine

12. **What does Minny do at the end of the book?**

    A. Moves in with Celia and Johnny
    B. Moves to New York City
    C. Leaves her abusive husband
    D. Becomes a writer

13. **Happens to Aibileen at the end of the book?**

    A. She adopts Mae Mobley
    B. She is fired from Miss Leefolt's house
    C. She moves in with Minny
    D. She moves to New York City

14. **To whom does Skeeter pass on the Miss Myrna job?**

A. Minny
B. Aibileen
C. Gretchen
D. Hilly

15. **What is Hilly's final act of revenge toward Minny?**

A. Hilly makes sure that Minny's children will never have jobs
B. Hilly causes Minny to be fired from the Foote household
C. Hilly causes Minny's husband to be fired from his job
D. Hilly tells everyone about the Terrible Awful

16. **How does Hilly recognize Miss Leefolt's character in the book about the maids?**

A. Hilly recognized the description of the house
B. Aibileen noted that her employer had an L-shaped crack in her dining room table
C. Aibileen used Mae Mobley's name
D. Hilly recognized a conversation from last months' bridge club

17. **Why does Aibileen get fired from Miss Leefolt's house?**

A. Hilly accuses her of stealing her silver
B. Mister Leefolt hears her telling her secret stories to Mae Mobley
C. Aibileen tells Miss Leefolt that she is a terrible mother
D. Miss Leefolt hears her telling her secret stories to Mae Mobley

18. **What hobby does Celia take up at the end of the book?**

A. Sewing
B. Hunting
C. Gardening
D. Cooking

19. **At the church celebration for Aibileen, what gift does the congregation give her?**

A. A copy of Help, signed by everyone in the black community of Jackson
B. A stained glass window in her name
C. A copy of the Bible, signed by everyone in the black community of Jackson
D. A laurel and a hearty handshake

20. **What momentous decision does Skeeter's mother make towards the end of the book?**

A. She decides to apologize to Lulabelle
B. She decides to adopt a black child
C. She decides not to die
D. She decides to re-hire Constantine

21. **Who replaces Constantine as the maid at the Phelan household?**

A. Aibileen
B. Pascagoula
C. Minny
D. Louvenia

22. **What does Minny's husband threaten to do to her after he loses his job?**

A. Desert the family
B. Kill Kindra
C. Lock her in the bathroom and set the house on fire
D. Divorce her

23. **At the very end of the book, why does Aibileen suggest that Hilly is in a prison of her own making?**

A. Hilly cannot let herself love anyone
B. She will spend the rest of her life trying to convince people that she did not eat that pie
C. No one talks to Hilly anymore
D. Everyone secretly hates her, but no one wants to tell her

24. **When questioned by Mr. Leefolt, who does Mae Mobley say she learned about anti-segregation activism from?**

A. The TV
B. Aibileen
C. Her mother
D. Miss Taylor

25. **What will Minny's children do now that she has left their father?**

A. Live with Sugar, the oldest child
B. Live with their mother
C. Live with their father
D. We don't know

Quiz 4 Answer Key

1. **(A)** Leroy
2. **(B)** Five
3. **(A)** Aibileen
4. **(C)** Stay out of her business
5. **(B)** Skeeter makes a "mistake" in the League newsletter asking people to drop off their used toilets
6. **(B)** Contribute it to the college fund for Yule May's sons
7. **(A)** Sorrow that Aibileen will lose her job
8. **(D)** Skeeter tells him about the book she is writing with the maids
9. **(A)** Help
10. **(A)** The Benefit
11. **(D)** To move to New York City and work for Harper's Magazine
12. **(C)** Leaves her abusive husband
13. **(B)** She is fired from Miss Leefolt's house
14. **(B)** Aibileen
15. **(C)** Hilly causes Minny's husband to be fired from his job
16. **(B)** Aibileen noted that her employer had an L-shaped crack in her dining room table
17. **(A)** Hilly accuses her of stealing her silver
18. **(C)** Gardening
19. **(A)** A copy of Help, signed by everyone in the black community of Jackson
20. **(C)** She decides not to die
21. **(B)** Pascagoula
22. **(C)** Lock her in the bathroom and set the house on fire
23. **(B)** She will spend the rest of her life trying to convince people that she did not eat that pie
24. **(D)** Miss Taylor
25. **(D)** We don't know

The Help Bibliography

Alexandra Nichipor, author of ClassicNote. Completed on September 4, 2015, copyright held by GradeSaver.

Updated and revised by Aaron Suduiko October 28, 2015. Copyright held by GradeSaver.

Williams, Juan. Bond, Julian.. Eyes on the Prize: America's Civil Rights Years, 1954-1965. . New York, NY: Penguin Books, 1987.

Stockett, Kathryn.. The Help. New York: Berkley, 2011.

Maslin, Janet. "Racial Insults and Quiet Bravery in 1960s Mississippi." *The New York Times*. The New York Times, 18 Feb. 2009. Web. 06 Sept. 2015. <http://www.nytimes.com/2009/02/19/books/19masl.html?_r=0>.

Duchess Harris . "Kathryn Stockett Is Not My Sister and I Am Not Her Help." The Feminist Wire. 8/12/2011. 8/15/2015. <http://www.thefeministwire.com/2011/08/kathryn-stockett-is-not-my-sister-and-i-am-not-her-help/>.

Printed in Great Britain
by Amazon

34472754R00070